# The Complete Book of
# MOTOCROSS

## by
## Frank Melling

*Foulis*

Haynes

**ISBN 0 85429 473 2**

© Frank Melling
First published June 1986

**A FOULIS Motorcycling book**
**Published by:**
**Haynes Publishing Group,**
Sparkford, Nr. Yeovil, Somerset, BA22 7JJ, England

**Haynes Publications Inc,**
**861, Lawrence Drive, Newbury Park, California, 91320. USA**

**British Library Cataloguing in Publication Data**

Melling, Frank
  The complete book of motocross
  1.  Motocross
  I.  Title
  796.7'5    GV1060.12

  ISBN 0-85429-473-2

**Library of Congress Catalog Card Number**

**86-80520**

Editor: **Jeff Clew**
Cover design: **Phill Jennings**
Page layout: **Chris Hull**
Printed in England by: J.H. Haynes & Co. Ltd.

Dust jacket photograph of Honda-mounted 1985 World 500 cc Motocross Champion Dave Thorpe

# Foreword

I get asked to write a lot of forewords for books and I always have to refuse. The reason for this is simple. As World Champion, everything I am associated with has to be the best. My bikes, clothing and equipment all have to be top quality, otherwise it shows me in a bad light. I agreed to write this foreword because I think that this book is the best of its kind.

More than anything else, any book which sets out to try and teach beginners has to be trustworthy. The writer has got to be accurate and thorough otherwise riders who don't have enough experience to know better can be led astray. Frank Melling knows a lot about motocross. He's been involved in the sport for 21 years both as a rider, a journalist and a team manager at every level from club meetings to Grands Prix and has a breadth of knowledge that few other writers can equal.

He's also clever enough to know what he doesn't know! A lot of the factory riders have helped him with the chapters on Grand Prix riding and machine preparation and there's plenty in these sections that even expert riders can learn.

Even though it's packed with information, the book is very easy and relaxing to read. Frank writes in a friendly, informal way which makes even difficult subjects easy to understand, which is great for young riders.

But the main reason I have agreed to be associated with this book is that Frank is the ultimate professional when it comes to writing. He cares about his books as much as I care about winning the World Championship — and that's a lot! I have enjoyed helping him with this book; I hope that you get as much pleasure from reading it as I did. Maybe I'll see you at a G.P. one day.

Best wishes.

*Graham Noyce*

# Acknowledgements

In producing any book, an author needs much help and support which it is often impossible to acknowledge formally. Many apparently small things can combine to become a major problem if they are not solved by helpful hands.

I am grateful to Alex Hodgkinson for his comments on G.P. motocross and to Doug Hacking motorcycles, Pendle Garages, C. D. Bramhall and Warrington trailers for their help with the section on vans and trailers.

Ray Meakin provided invaluable technical support with the photography whilst Malcolm Kent, of Alfred G. Taylor (Liverpool) persuaded me that I ought to go "electronic" for this book. Learning the vagaries of word processing equipment was as hard as mastering racing but well worth the effort. How did we manage before discs?

# Contents

# A guide to the contents

**Chapter One: If it moves – race it!**
In this first chapter, we look at how motocross began with road bike "scrambles" and how it grew into an international sport. Jeff Smith, Joel Robert and Roger de Coster are all to be found here.

**Chapter Two: The rise and fall of the professional**
Now we look at motocross as the professional sport it is today. You can find out in Chapter two how much the Japanese really spend on racing and how modern rear suspension came about.

**Chapter Three: Clothing**
Chapter three is all about clothing. We talk about jeans, boots, helmets, gloves and body armour and think about the problems of buying cheap riding gear which wears out very quickly.

**Chapter Four: Buying a bike**
In chapter four one of the cleverest buyers of second-hand bikes talks about the tricks of the trade. He will tell you how to buy a second-hand bike and not get stuck with a heap of junk. We will also think about the good and bad things when buying a bike from a dealer or from another rider.

**Chapter Five: Caring for the beast**

> Now we have got a bike, we've got to look after it! Chapter five is all about bike maintenance. It tells you about buying and using the right tools, cleaning the bike and preparing it for the next race.

**Chapter Six: Tuning**

> Chapter six is for all those riders who want to tune their bikes. A top Grand Prix mechanic tells you all the secrets of tuning the motor and the suspension. Some of the work requires a lot of skill but it will make your bike go quicker and handle better.

**Chapter Seven: Tyres and tyre fitting**

> Tyres are now so important that they have chapter seven all to themselves. We look at the difference between hard, soft and intermediate tyres for different tracks and how to fit tyres. There is also a chart so you will know the best size tyre to fit to your bike.

**Chapter Eight: Getting to the meeting**

> Chapter eight talks about getting your bike to the meeting. We look at buying a second-hand van and building a trailer.

**Chapter Nine: Race fit**

> The whole of chapter nine is about physical fitness. First, we look at Kurt Nicoll's training programme. If you can do this, you will be fit enough to race in a Grand Prix. A top surgeon talks about the different injuries from which a rider can suffer.

**Chapter Ten: Joining a club**

> All motocross racers have to be in a club. Chapter ten tells you how to join a club and which organization is the best for you to ride with. It talks about schoolboy racing, getting entry forms and insurance.

**Chapter Eleven: Riding techniques**

> If you are just starting riding, chapter eleven is the most important for you to read. It tells you how to ride a motocross bike uphill and downhill as well as on the flat, and how to jump the bike.

**Chapter Twelve: Ready to race**

> Chapter twelve tells you all the things you need to know before you start racing. It tells you what to take to a race, where to park, what to do when you get to the track and how to practise.

**Chapter Thirteen: Racing!**

> If you want to be a super-star, then read chapter thirteen. Some of the world's top riders helped with this section and they tell you how to do double jumps, "handbrake turns" and how to make the holeshot every time you start. All the secrets of Grand Prix racing are here.

**Chapter Fourteen: Sponsorship**

> If you want a motorhome like Dave Thorpe or just some free stickers, chapter fourteen tells you how to get them. It also talks about the bad things as well as the good things in being sponsored.

**Chapter Fifteen: A week in the life of a champion**

> If you want to know what Dave Thorpe is really like, read chapter fifteen. Dave tells you all about a whole week in his life – the training, meeting the press and the racing. You'll really know all about the World Champion after reading this.

# Introduction

There are many reasons for writing a book. The lure of money — more imagined than real in the case of most authors — the satisfaction of a mammoth ego boost as you see **your** book on sale to the public for the first time and the need to quench a deep-rooted creative desire to elucidate a theory, or influence opinion, are all powerful motivators.

Each of these elements have affected the production of *The Complete Book of Motocross*. Yes, I do want to make some money from the book and I will be ecstatic if the finished product is as Editor Jeff Clew, and myself, have envisaged. Sales of 100,000 copies too, will be greeted with equal enthusiasm. I will also be pleased if my ideas prove to be worthy of consideration by others, for there is more than a little of the messiah in most of us.

However, none of these reasons is the primary one for writing this book. More than anything else, I wanted to say "thank you" to the sport which has given me so much over the years.

This will be the last "how to do it" motocross book that I can write. After 21 years of racing, I am now too old to compete seriously and I will soon lose that critical empathy with the racer's mind which comes not only from being with riders in the paddock but also wheel to wheel with them on the track. A good motocross book demands not only knowledge and enthusiasm on the part of the writer but also the tightening of the gut as a passing manoeuvre is described and a shared sense of pride in the cheap, and often ugly, trophy won by a third placed Junior in his first season. You have not only to know motocross but also to love it — shamelessly and openly — if you are to capture its magnificent spirit in words.

This year, I won the 250 class at a beach race and nearly wrote the van off on the way home through stealing glances at my trophy — a fine example of plastic and aluminium *art grotto*. Here truly, was *Mudgrunt Vulgaris* in action: one hand clutching a beef sandwich, the other loosely wrapped round the steering wheel and both eyes firmly fixed on the booty: bursting with pride and a danger to every other road user.

And *Mudgrunt* I surely am and proud to be so. Yet, through good fortune, limitless hard work and a boundless enthusiasm for racing bikes off-road I went from 3 last places in the Oswestry Club's 1964 Spring Scramble to a career which gave me a factory G.P. bike from BSA, rides all over Europe and America and the friendship of a vast range of the world best motocross racers. It has been a long trip for a naive teenager, whose highest ambition in life was to make the top 20 of Cheshire Centre heat and whose dearest dream was to qualify for a final just once.

To he who controls all our destinies, I say, "thank you". The broken bones, the hospital beds and the physiotherapy were not exactly welcome but they, and the perennially exasperated letters from the bank manager about my racing excesses were a fair exchange for what I have received. Yes, I have had a very fair deal.

I hope that the reader will tolerate these rather self-indulgent musings confident that this will be the only place in the book in which they appear. Let me conclude by saying that motocross is a hard mistress. Expensive to maintain and physically demanding. Enjoy every minute of her whilst you can and never look back with regret when she casts you aside for the attention of a new, younger rider.

So to this book. My first *Ride It! The Complete Book of Motocross* was a top

*Mudgrunt Vulgaris* **at play**.

selling motorcycle title in the Haynes' list and an international best seller. It was a hard act to follow not only in terms of sales but also because motocross had changed. In 1973, when *Motocross* was being written, it was possible for one person — with the help of a few knowledgeable friends — to possess the experience necessary to completely master the sport. Hence, in the first book, it is usual that my opinion is the one which is quoted. My ideas were checked and stimulated by expert advice but basically, I knew 75% of that book's content from my own experience. In the 10 years between writing the two books, I became even more knowledgeable but ironically, the sport expanded and became so complex so quickly that when I came to write the new book, I found that rather than having the answers to hand, I was only in position construct an outline and then ask the **questions** which would hopefully lead to the correct answers. Motocross is now a field where expert knowledge is essential. The top rider rarely works on his own bike and the mechanic doesn't touch the rear shock or front forks — that is the rôle of the shock technician. Every team has its own portable computer where the tactics of the opposition's training are analysed through their lap times whilst in the background, the tyre designers offer ever increasingly subtle tread and compounds to gain the extra milli-second of advantage.

To write a motocross book now, all these experts must be consulted, for their

knowledge literally represents the "state of the art". Unfortunately, because they are so expert, and work at the highest levels of the motocross industry, their expertise needs re-organising into a more palatable form before it is of any use to the average rider. Whilst testing ten different rear tyres is the right thing to do if one wishes to have the optimum choice for a track, it is hardly a sensible recommendation for the rider who has spent his last six weeks trying to save up enough to purchase just one tyre — of any type!

Because I can still look at motocross through the eyes of the ordinary club racer I have been able to ask the questions he, and increasingly she as well, will want to resolve. My knowledge of the sport has enabled me to interpret the information I have been given and to organize and present it in a form which I hope is useful, interesting and a pleasure to read.

Throughout the book, I have tried to be meticulous in giving credit to those many experts who have helped me. Too often, authors and journalists will demand information which exists only in the mind of one person, take it for their own use and then scarcely stop to whisper a word of thanks. I am very grateful to all those who helped me in any way, great or small, and I am particularly anxious to thank everyone for tolerating my demands not only for information but for that of **very best** quality it was possible for them to provide. Time and again, I have faced the embarrassing situation of having to 'phone someone, or write to them, thanking them for their help but asking for more detail and greater clarification. I do not claim that every single piece of information in the 70,000 odd words which appear in this book is perfect, only that it is the very best which could be produced by me at the time of writing.

This then brings us to a few people who have been more than helpful — their assistance has been essential and without it, the book would be much the poorer. In random order, the first mention goes to Kurt Nicoll and Dave Watson. Kurt hates books and reading (except for the bottom line of contract) and so his efforts — usually willing and sometimes smiling — were a great credit to his courage. It's all over now, Kurt, so the headaches will go away. In Dave Watson, I was privileged to work with one of the most thoughtful and articulate of Grand Prix riders. It is always worth listening to David and I enjoyed many stimulating conversations which shaped the book directly and indirectly. Dave Thorpe gave his help whenever it was needed and provided some of the easiest work of the book. If it was humanly possible to do it, then Dave would. Further, whatever the task, it was carried out with courtesy, dignity and sheer good humour. Overall, the most professional rider with whom I have worked since Roger De Coster. Rob Hooper cast his critical and forthright eye over the book. Never one to flatter an author, praise from Rob always made me feel that the chapter was reaching the standards of excellence both he and I wanted. Finally, I must mention Neil Hudson. Modest to the point of acute shyness, Neil was overwhelmingly helpful with the section on riding techniques, throughout which he never claimed he really knew much about riding at all. Still technically one of the finest riders in the world, Neil is also one of the nicest persons in motocross.

Capturing the action and style of all these riders has been a challenging task. Mark Price and I tackled the job together, with the bulk of the work falling to Mark. He used a brilliant technical skill and an empathy with motocross which makes him one of Europe's top sports photographers and the book would be much poorer without his contributions. I used a lot of film.

Help came from many sources in the trade and all of it of the highest possible calibre. Stuart Wyss of Dunlop provided the sort of product knowledge and organization that one dreams of receiving just once in a lifetime and Dave Fennel was equally enthusiastic about the Clover clothing of which he is so justly proud. Bill Brown's vast and perceptive knowledge of motorcycle retailing was invaluable.

At this time I was working for Rock Oil, and this put Works Manager, Charles Hewitt, in a difficult position. First, he was living with the programme as long as me and had to provide the sort of encouragement that all authors need when the going gets heavy. He did this well and also responded positively to my requests to go and check out various Grand Prix scattered around Europe which by sheer coincidence also helped my research tremendously.

The last word must go to Eddie Crooks, the owner of my present bike. There is nothing to say about Ed. except that he is the best sponsor in the world — bar none. When I have won for him — and that doesn't happen much these days — the sole reason for my success is my riding ability. If I don't do well, it's because the bike isn't good enough. Eddie is a fine sponsor and first-class friend. I have determined that my last ride will be on a Crooks-Suzuki because in riding for Ed., one is riding for the best — the very best.

The book is not dedicated to any of my friends or to some one mentor who has influenced my writing or racing. Rather, I have tried to write a really complete book of motocross for you, all the *Mudgrunts and Mudgruntesses* who make the sport what it is. I hope that you will have at least half the enjoyment I have had from motocross. If you do, then you can look back on time well spent.

Frank Melling — September 1985

**The author and his close friend, Neil Hudson, working on this book together.**

# If it moves - race it!

It wasn't too long after the birth of the first motorcycle that stalwart souls began to race these new, agile mechanical beasts. The first race of any note to be held particularly for motorcycles was in 1904, on the outskirts of Paris, and some ten years later, Alfred Scott arranged what was the earliest cross-country competition, as a form of relaxation for his employees at the famous Scott motorcycle factory.

The descendant of this event, still adhering very much to its original format, lives on today as the Scott trial and true to form, it is a time and observation event taking in some severe areas of the Yorkshire moors and providing just as much of a challenge now. Enthusiasts of the day came to admire Alfred Scott's trials and by 1923 there was sufficient interest in rough riding for the Camberley Club, some two hundred miles to the south of Scott's capers, to consider running a speed hill climb on Camberley Heath.

The event was not a great success and seems to have generated little enthusiasm in either the press or riders, even though the legendary Gus Kuhn set some spectacular times on a Velocette single equipped with a tyreless, but studded, rear rim. The club was not daunted by this setback and within a few months they had decided to try something more ambitious — this time embodying the more desirable aspects of the Scott Trial. Then, as now, the speed sections were what interested the Camberley Club men.

Camberley Heath in Surrey was the venue and a course was laid out which included two fierce hills and a three mile long straight, permitting those competitors who could avoid the potholes, and survive the bumps, to exceed 65 mph. Fast even by today's standards, this must have been horrific in 1924.

The racers were expected to cover two laps — one in the morning and one in the afternoon — and the fastest aggregate time won overall; in other words, a two leg motocross event! The exact length of the course is not known but it must have been at least thirty miles a lap and the competitors attacked it in full touring gear consisting of a cloth cap, riding breeches, storm coat and a thick scarf. However, by the end of the meeting we are assured by the journalists of the day that many of the more serious racers had stripped down to more basic apparel.

Determination was the key word for all concerned and by the close of the meeting, headlamps, exhaust pipes and all other detachable accessories which make up a road-going motorcycle formed a thick layer around the course. The men were exhausted and the bikes shattered – things haven't changed much – and Mr A. B. Sparks, the gallant rider of a 496cc Scott was estatic in the March mist at having won the very first Southern Scott Scramble.

"Scramble" – a new word – was born, one which described the cavorting of men and machines under the most strenuous of conditions. The English, with customary panache for understatement, described the horrific scene as "a bit of a scramble".

**R. B. Budd has difficulty in keeping the front wheel of his AJS on the ground after cresting Red Road during the first Southern Scott scramble.**

The embryo sport continued to grow until the second World War put a stop to most sporting activities, except those practised round the back of the NAAFI. During this period, scrambles machines were extremely close relatives of the ones our grandfathers rode to work. There were "sports" models offered, but the period immediately prior to 1939 was really the hey-day of the ride-the-bike-to-the-meetering enthusiast, the idea being to use the same machine for both road and track.

I often hear riders who competed under these conditions lament the "spoilt" modern competitors who have specially prepared machines just to race. I don't know that I fully agree with the concept of today's riders being pampered but I would certainly relish the idea of riding my Suzuki to meetings. Full lock slides through queues of cars, and hundred mile wheelies from the traffic lights would really be some fun. A hundred and fifty riders, all nicely tensed up for the forthcoming races, would do no end of good for motorcycling's public image as they all made their way sedately to the track. The traffic police would have a field day!

After the war, the development of motocross bikes as we would recognise them today, began in earnest. Matchless perfected a telescopic front fork which revolutionised front suspension. In fact, the *Teledraulic* fork, as it was called, had an action which is still good by modern standards, and in its day, it must have been quite a revelation. Swinging arm suspension soon followed and where it wasn't supplied in a suitable form by the manufacturers, private owners practised their own skills, much as 1973 saw every able-bodied welder called in to 'improve' handling by moving the rear dampers all over the frame.

Motocross was now truly international with serious, and successful, entries from most European countries. In the early 1950s, Britain ruled supreme with such formidable competitors as Basil Hall, Les Archer and John Draper, while Belgium provided the main opposition with the redoubtable Auguste Mingels and Rene Baeten. The riders of this period were really men of fire and iron. They had to be, for by comparison with our bikes their equipment was extremely crude. Every competitive bike was powered by a heavy 500cc single cylinder four-stroke engine and frames were built to withstand both the power and weight of these formidable engines. There were exceptions, for even as early as 1956, Les Archer won the then European championship on a home-brewed special, powered by a long stroke ohc Manx Norton engine housed in a chassis which made some attempt at lightness and balance.

I raced these bikes when I first started riding and they are really light years apart from a modern motocross machine. Without going into great depth, I still remember the care with which the bike had to be set up for jumps and corners. Every action was very much premeditated and the penalty was usually severe for trying to flick the machine about as one would ride a modern bike. Having experienced just how much of a handful these "real bikes" were, I am repeatedly left in silent admiration when I see pictures of Tibblin, Archer, Smith and the rest, throwing their mounts about as if they were the latest offering from the Honda factory.

With the FIM acknowledgement that the 250 cc class could provide worthwhile racing by granting a European Championship in 1957, progress towards today's lightweight machines began to speed up. The two-stroke engine, because it was lighter, and also because it was less powerful, could be housed in a lighter chassis and this meant much better handling over rough going.

*Above:* **Jeff Smith leads the field on a 499cc Gold Star BSA at Hawkstone Park on 20th March 1960. John Clayton and Dave Curtis follow in his wake.**

*Below:* **Jeff Smith on the titanium frame 494cc BSA during its first outing in the 1966 Hants Grand National.**

For many years, the four-stroke machine made up for the ease of handling by sheer power. It is worth remembering that a good 500 cc four-stroke in 1960, was quicker over a quarter mile than any two-stroke until as late, probably, as 1971. In the 1960s a Villiers based 250 cc engine, producing something around 18 bhp and with a not very inspiring gearbox, would not see which way most 500s were going. Yet despite the power advantage, the signs were clear — especially in the 500 cc class — that handling was of paramount importance and BSA were the factory to realise this and do something about it.

BSA's story is worth a book in itself for it is a tale of one of the most formidable teams ever to be gathered together in the motocross world, yet who statistically achieved so little. Two World Championships came to the factory in 1964 and 1965 through the efforts of Jeff Smith but this in no way indicates the stranglehold in which they held British, and to a lesser extent, European motocross. In addition to Smith's two World Championships, John Banks was runner up to the brilliant East German, Paul Friedrichs on two occasions. His son Mark is now about to begin his own pursuit of the 500 cc World Championship crown.

Although they did win an immense number of races, the team seemed always to be dogged with bad luck when it really counted. Jerry Scott, a rider who was faster than Jeff Smith on occasions, and surely destined to become World Champion, was tragically killed at Thirsk. Vic Eastwood left the team because of an internal squabble, and after being chosen as Husqvarna team leader, suffered very bad injuries to his leg when he fell on a frozen track and was run over at Hawkstone Park. In 1970, Vic Allen was one of the fastest men in the motocross world and seemed a certain World Champion. He fell in the first moto of the Italian Grand Prix, breaking his leg, and by the time he had recovered, the team had been disbanded through the hapless blunder of an accountant.

It is a tragic story offset only by the innumerable technical advances achieved at a time when progress was being made in leaps and bounds. BSA were the first to use a lightweight four-stroke engine in the 500 cc class — a 420 cc version of the 350 cc B40, itself a derivative of the ubiquitous C15. On this bike, Smith won his first world title in 1964, despite a gearbox which was held together by hope and a prayer. In the following year, Smith won again, this time on a 440 cc version of the engine which by now was more reliable.

Two years later, a full 494 cc engine has been produced and by April 1966, the BSA had reached its highest state of sophistication, if not success, with a magnesium engine, titanium frame and fork sliders and a rear disc brake — a machine five years ahead of its time. Virtually the same motor, in a Cheney chassis but certainly no more refined than the BSAs, although perhaps steering a little better, carried John Banks to third place overall in the 1973 Grand Prix at Carlsbad, USA, a fair indication of just how good the BSA was at the time of its conception.

Regardless of how many technical advances the team made, or the number of races they won, the management was always distant from the Competition Department. There is no denying that both parties preferred the relationship this way, but when the BSA group hit financial trouble in 1971, there was no one to plead the comp. shop's case when the accountant's axe fell. In a few months, what had taken two decades to build was ruthlessly and haphazardly smashed. So clumsy was the destruction that by January 1972, Group PRO, Reg Dancer, felt sufficiently moved to tell me that even top management regretted the wholesale slaughter and dearly wished that the race shop had only been pruned and not annihilated. It was too late. Banks had gone to Husqvarna, Smith to Canada developing motocross and trail machines for Can-Am, Allan was about to join Bultaco and Brian Martin – the brilliant team manager and co-ordinator of the whole BSA motocross effort – was now a sales representative selling road machines. A tragic end to one of the world's dynamic teams.

Meanwhile, in the 250 cc class, Husqvarna and CZ were engaged in a relentless battle for superiority. To name the factories does not convey the mood of the time, for it was not Husqvarna and CZ who were locked in combat but Torsten Hallman and Joel Robert. In the ten seasons from 1962 to 1972, these two riders dominated the world 250 cc class and with the sole exception of 1965, when the neat and exceptionally fast Russian, Victor Arbekov, took the crown, one of them was World Champion every year.

**Jeff Smith and Brian Martin working on the 494cc BSA in the paddock. Apart from the frame, titanium was also used for the fork sliders. With a magnesium engine and rear hydraulic disc brake, the ready-to-race weight of the machine was lower than that of the best 250s of the day.**

It is worth mentioning Arbekov because in many ways he epitomized both the strength and weakness of Russian motocross. A superbly fit athlete, who could race the whole 45 minutes without a trace of tiredness, he was also very neat and apparently without fear. In 1965, he outrode both Hallman and Robert, bringing great honour to Russia. Incredibly, he was rewarded by being taken from his family to some remote training camp and there put through the most gruelling programme of riding and physical training during the winter. Without a break from

riding or training for 18 months, Arbekov arrived at the start of the 1966 season tired, morose and dejected — totally without any motivation to retain his title. He faded from the motocross scene very quickly and the last we heard of this fine rider was that he was teaching motocross in East Germany and no doubt enjoying this job infinitely more than facing the traumas of another World Championship success.

Meanwhile, Joel Robert and Torsten Hallman battled it out. Robert, the flamboyant, whiskey-drinking clown, always to be seen with a cigarette in his mouth and a smile on his face, contrasted sharply with Hallman — a much quieter character who relied as much on brain power for his racing as he did on physical fitness.

**The author aboard a 250cc Cheney Suzuki fitted with the Olle Pettersson G.P. engine.**

Other factories, such as Greeves, who sent a host of British riders including Dave Bickers, John Griffiths, Alan Clough and John Done to compete in Grands Prix, contested the World Championships but they were always left in the shadow of the two Titans. Hallman was neat and polished, seeming to expend the minimum of effort in guiding his bike round the track, whilst Robert rode in a permanent tangle relying on a breathtaking sense of timing to sort out the most potentially dangerous situations. Hallman drove round corners with both wheels in line – Robert drifted through the same bends in a flat- out power slide. Hallman jumped straight and low – Robert was airborne long enough to qualify as an aircraft and landed on whichever part of the bike hit the ground first. So it went on, with Robert winning three world titles on a CZ and Hallman taking four on the Husqvarna up to 1969, when Robert moved to Suzuki and Hallman began to decline.

The season of 1968, the year before Robert left CZ, was an important one, for it marked the first serious presence of the Japanese in motocross. Up to this time it had been possible for very small factories to race in Grands Prix for quite modest outlays. For example, Husqvarna's 1959 250 cc Grand Prix bike, which successfully took the world title, was a close relative of the Silver Arrow road bike. It had a three speed engine unit giving around 16 bhp and although the machine had competition- orientated leading link forks and lightweight hubs, it was still a relatively simple motorcycle. Husqvarna's 500 cc entrant the same year was even more conservative since this engine was based on a design by Folke Mannerstedt executed in 1935. Even so, the machine was the best in the world and with Rolf Tibblin in the saddle, captured the European Championship for that year.

In the following eight years, much progress was made. BSA, as we have seen, forced the pace in the 500 cc class with their pioneering use of lightweight engines and frames and CZ, Greeves and Husqvarna all reached the stage where they could produce fast, reliable two stroke engines. However, in 1969, when Robert won his last World Championship for CZ, he arrived at meetings towing his own bike on a home- made trailer and Torsten Hallman was still expected to do his part in machine preparation. A good works' contract was considered to provide a couple of bikes and free spares together with the occasional bonus for winning a National Championship. Only the exclusive few took home substantial pay packets from the factory and out of this they were expected to finance their own activities.

The manufacturers who contested the World Championship did so primarily to sell competition motorcycles – replicas of the bikes used in the Grands Prix. Their production capacity was small and their budgets limited and every one accepted the status quo and adjusted their values accordingly. Suzuki changed all this. Here was a factory producing a greater number of any model in their range of vehicles than the combined output of every motocross factory in the rest of the world. The racing budget was limitless, the research facilities infinite, and the desire to win, all consuming.

In 1967, the Suzuki technicians came with cameras and notebooks. In 1968, Olle Pettersson – an ex- Husqvarna rider and Grand Prix runner, if not a leading contender – was signed to develop a competitive motocross machine, whilst in Britain, a parallel programme was carried out under the enthusiastic auspices of Suzuki (GB) boss, Alan Kimber. The Pettersson bike consistently managed to obtain good placings, finishing 7th in the world ratings. A year later, Olle took the improved machine, now known as the RH69, to third place in the World

Championship.

In England, Kimber had decided to cut corners by commissioning Eric Cheney to build a chassis for Pettersson's "old" Grand Prix engine and this was completed in the winter of 1968. Shortly afterwards, a new unit was sent from Japan along with fresh Grand Prix motors for Pettersson and it was on this bike that Tom Leadbitter, now better known for his speedway activities, set the motocross world on its ear by annihilating a top class entry in the Nantwich Television Scramble. Although Leadbitter did not win the race, he led the whole of the BSA team including the then prospective World Champion, John Banks, in addition to every other British expert, for most of the race. This had tremendous impact since at the time BSA were considered to be absolutely impregnable in British meetings.

I did a track test of the bike for *Cycle Illustrated*, an American magazine, and it impressed me at the time as a really outstanding motorcycle. Cheney produced a slim, lightweight chassis with a teardrop-shaped petrol tank which further added to the grace and beauty of the bike. Aesthetics apart, it went well too, although hindered somewhat by a narrow power band. At the time, there was talk of marketing replicas of the bike for around £350 — some hundred pounds or so below the Husqvarnas which were dominating the scene in 1968/69 — but the scheme was lost when Suzuki GB got into financial trouble and were taken over by the Lambretta Concessionaires. In any case, Suzuki had a much more interesting project.

In buying Robert's services, the Hamamatsu factory had secured the best 250 cc rider in the world. Knowing this, they set about building him the best motocross machine ever seen by attacking the root source of all evil; weight! Reduce weight and handling is vastly improved. Reduce weight and rider fatigue is dramatically lessened. Reduce weight and acceleration increases.

In 1970, Robert won the World Championship convincingly, although the bike was less than perfect, winning seven motos in four Grands Prix. His team mate, Sylvain Geboers, an exceptional rider who had the misfortune to be second string to the finest 250 cc rider in the world, won six motos at the Belgian, Russian and Polish rounds. Thus, not only did Robert take home the world crown, but Suzuki also captured the manufacturer's award.

If 1970 was a good season for the Japanese factory, it was but a pale imitation of the following year. Roger de Coster was brought in to have an exploratory attempt at the fiercely competitive 500 cc class and surpassed everyone's expectations by winning the World Championship and contributing heavily to Suzuki's annexation of the manufacturer's award. Robert did the same in the 250 cc class and so Suzuki won all four major motocross awards — a truly incredible feat.

Remarkable as Suzuki's effort was, it also had its darker side, for the Japanese GP bikes had reached such a state of sophistication that they really had no competitors. Yamaha and Kawasaki, the latter having hired the evergreen Olle Pettersson as development rider, were making tentative attempts at serious motocross racing but other than these two giants, there was no other company in the motocross world with sufficient funds to build the titanium and aluminium alloy frames which Suzuki utilised for their incredibly light bikes.

Husqvarna did try — and came near to financial disaster in the attempt. Many others, such as Bultaco, simply did not bother and concentrated on making good production bikes for sale to the general public. Suzuki raced primarily for publicity

**Graham Noyce in his Maico days – beautifully fluent and aggressive.**

to sell their huge range of road machines whilst the European manufacturers raced for publicity to sell racing bikes. With sales exceeding a million units each year the Japanese would always have the whip hand over companies who were delighted if they managed 15,000 bikes in a season. Then for once in its chequered and oft criticised career, the sporting committee of the FIM made a really worthwhile change in the rules governing motocross. Henceforth, they proclaimed, all machines racing in the 250 cc class shall not weigh less than 90 kg (198 lb) and in the 500 cc class, the bikes must not weigh less than 95 kg (209 lb). This ruling radically changed the face of motocross for now the emphasis was placed on handling, not merely weight reduction, and the ball was firmly back in the court of the small manufacturer with tiny, but very knowledgeable, development teams.

In the three years that Suzuki had dominated world motocross, much of the sophisticated knowledge needed to produce competitive motocross engines had filtered through to the smaller manufacturers. Some of this knowledge had been acquired quite legitimately through engineering papers published on two-stroke design or merely the absorption and development of new techniques. Other information arrived in plain vans in the early hours of the morning, for a surprising number of Japanese works bikes seemed to get diverted on their travels around Europe. The result of this free interchange of information was that any serious manufacturer could now build a competitive two-stroke racing engine for either the 250 or 500 class. The important difference now lay in handling and power delivery.

So it was in 1973 that Willi Bauer — a young German taking over from Åke Johnsson as Maico's team leader in the 500 cc class — came within one Grand Prix of taking the world title from de Coster and Suzuki, even though the Maico competition shop employed only half a dozen men compared with Suzuki's fifty plus. 1973 also saw Yamaha take the 250 cc world title with their bike using the controversial "*Monoshock*" rear suspension, although it is generally accepted that Hakan Andersson, not the *Monoshock*, was responsible for Yamaha's first Motocross World Championship. Certainly, despite massive publicity, it has since failed to achieve general acceptance, or good results, on any consistent basis.

The FIM ruling on weight had one other very dramatic effect on Grand Prix motocross — it temporarily brought about the return of the four-stroke engine. Two-strokes had totally dominated the World Championship scene after the demise of the BSA competition effort, but with a realistic minimum weight target, it was now possible for small manufacturers to have another go at GP racing.

This renewed effort was led by Eric Cheney, who supported John Banks in his full attempt at the world series, and proved once again that the four-stroke engine was competitive in Motocross. The effort was badly hampered by the lack of funds since grands prix racing is an extremely costly exercise both in terms of cash and time for a manufacturer as small as Cheney. Even so, good results — including a third place at Carlsbad — were achieved and had there been sufficient funds to have had a second try in 1974, he would surely have achieved even more.

Taking over as the sole four-stroke manufacturer represented in the 1974 series, Alan Clews soldiered on with his short-stroke CCM — a derivative of the old BSA power-plant. Although not blessed with the best of luck, John Banks, who switched camps after a disagreement with Cheney — did manage a fourth place at Luxembourg, a brave attempt from a back street manufacturer.

Conjecture is an interesting exercise but it must not detract from those who

**The first Kawasaki KX250 engine, campaigned by the ex-Suzuki works runner, Olle Pettersson.**

have earned their honour today, and in 1974, that honour belonged to Heikki Mikkola and his 360 cc Husqvarna and Jaroslav Falta who rode a works CZ to a moral victory, if not statistical, in the 250 cc Championship.

Husqvarna returned once again to the World Championship pinnacle with a clever 360 cc design by Rubin Helmin. The bike proved to be very quick and easy to ride but most of all, it was reliable. Whilst de Coster and his Suzuki were as fast, or even faster on occasions than the rival Husqvarna team, they were continually dogged by failures which cost them valuable points. Mikkola, on the other hand, never suffered one mechanical breakdown throughout the whole season and scored consistently, to break the Japanese stranglehold on motocross for the first time since Bengt Aberg's victory in 1970, once again aboard a Husqvarna. A well-earned victory and a vindication for Husqvarna's policy of racing the machine which formed the following year's production bike, rather than competing with special machines which would never be sold to the public.

Overshadowing Heikki Mikkola's fine performance in the 500 cc class was the sinister spectre of political motivation which tainted the 250 cc world series for on August 25th 1974, Jaroslav Falta was robbed of his first ever World Championship by Russian gamesmanship of the lowest type.

I was privileged, if this is the right term for so distasteful an experience, to be at Wohlen and personally witness the incidents which led up to the FIM jury penalizing Falta by one minute for unfair riding at the start, a vital minute which cost him victory in the second moto, and subsequently the vital points needed to take the World Championship.

The Russians, who were determined that Guennady Moisseev and his KTM would win at all costs, lodged an objection which alleged that Falta had made an unfair start. This should have been thrown out on two counts. Firstly, if Falta had cheated at the start then the race should have been stopped immediately and a fresh start declared. Therefore, if the race was continued the start must have been fair. Secondly, Falta's "crime" was to hit the metal starting gate with his front wheel in the air — a perfectly fair manoeuvre by motocross standards — and his rear wheel followed it down. If the young Czech had jumped the gate before it moved, then his CZ, with its low underslung exhaust, would have perched firmly on top and there would have been no argument about the matter. But nothing of the sort happened and Falta made a good, fast start, along with three or four other riders.

To compound the Russians' felony, they sent Victor Popenko out with what appeared to be the express intention of putting Falta out of the race. He very nearly did this on a slow downhill section of the course, which finished in a very tight hairpin bend, with sufficient room for only one machine to pass at a time at racing speeds. Here, Popenko seemed to ram Falta deliberately, bringing him off and pushing him into the ropes. The incident cost Falta some thirty seconds and he was then faced with the apparently impossible task of catching and passing Harry Everts, who had found dynamic form on the factory Puch.

At first, Falta's mechanics waved him on to keep going — he was so far behind that they did not even bother to time the gap. Then as the laps went by, Falta scythed through the field like a man possessed, which indeed, he was. The twenty second sign came up as Falta, his blue CZ shirt torn and bloodstained, flashed past the ever increasing group of CZ men and up the short hill on to the main straight and after the Puch of Everts. In a miraculously short time, '9 Everts', together with feverish waves and tearful pleadings from Falta's men, appeared on the gruby black plywood pit board and we knew then that Falta was going to win the race.

Falta, at his most dynamic and forceful best, swooped on the flying Everts like a greyhound on a rabbit. They passed the pits side by side, Falta on the inside line and Everts a few feet nearer the paddock and almost brushing the delerious mechanics who were encroaching further on to the track as each lap passed. In a style befitting a World Champion, Falta went past Everts in mid-air, changing up a gear as he did so. Everts, to his credit, tried to race the Czech even at this stage, but Falta brushed aside the challenge with almost contemptuous ease and went on to take the chequered flag.

Then came the protests and a weak FIM jury, who some observers say never even saw the start line incident, robbed Falta and CZ of what were rightfully theirs. The World Championship went instead to a pale, dejected husk of a man, Guennady Moisseev. The Russian showed none of his exciting riding style at Wohlen; none of the verve and skill which Russian motocross so often produces. Instead, he was a sad empty man who looked tired of motocross and fearful of the results of his riding – whether it be success or failure. Not content with the destruction of Arbekov, Russian or KTM tactics (for the Austrian factory was a prime mover in the making of the protest) they had destroyed the Soviet's second World Champion, far, far more effectively than any opponent could have done. It was a sad day for Moisseev; a sad day for KTM in encouraging the Russian action; a very sad day for what is the cleanest professional sport in the world.

In presenting this brief chronicle of motocross, I am conscious of having left out so much. The 1950s need two chapters to themselves as does the development of the CZ two-strokes. Then there was the hey-day of the Villiers-based scramblers which earned firms like Cotton, Dot and DMW a lasting place in the annals of motocross history. The story of Paul Friedrich's epic struggles with Jeff Smith and John Banks are worth twenty pages, as is the history of Husqvarna's all-conquering 400 cc bike. In recent times, the Spanish firms have produced some brilliant bikes and I am reluctant to dismiss Kalevi Vehekonen's exploits on the Montesa, but the line has to be drawn somewhere.

# The rise and
# fall of the professional

I make no apologies for including the preceding chapter in this new book for it was, and is, a good summary of the first fifty years of the sport. Working on a reed-valved, water-cooled 125, there might seem to be little value in hearing the exploits of ageing heroes and obsolete bikes. However, I have always been fond of a Chinese proverb — itself hardly fresh off the production line — attributed to a warlord who died 4,000 years ago: "We need to know the past in order to understand the present and predict the future."

So it is with motocross. Giving some thought to the mistakes of others might be a way of avoiding them oneself. Certainly, as I write these words in 1984, there are a lot of manufacturers starting to think very seriously about their involvement in motocross and they are beginning to question its validity.

The reason for this is cost. I left the last book at 1974, when the whole sport was peaking towards an ecstatic crest. Bikes could be sold as fast as they were made. The oil crisis had not hit us. Employment was high throughout the Western world and the American market had an apparently insatiable desire for the very best motocross manufacturers could supply. These factors, plus the pride all companies feel in success, were to draw all four Japanese manufacturers into total warfare — particularly in the prestigious 500 cc class.

To conduct an efficient war, generals need the best troops and the best equipment and in neither sphere did the Japanese leave themselves short. In fact, G.P. racing in the 500 cc class became so intense that every other country involved in motorcycle manufacture could make only a token contribution. Perhaps this is being somewhat hard on the Europeans for often the attempt was more successful than the word "token" implies. Maico certainly provided opposition first with Adolf Weil, then Willi Bauer and finally Graham Noyce, whilst in the 250 class — a capacity which has never held more than a passing interest for

**Roger de Coster, who won his first World Championship in 1971.**

the Japanese —both KTM and Husqvarna produced World Champions.

However, whilst no-one could decry the efforts of both the riders and manufacturers of this class, the fastest men and most sophisticated machinery were always in the 500 cc division. Consequently a chicken and egg situation arose. Because of the quality of the racing, the media tended to concentrate on the 500 cc class. Thus, it became even more prestigious, attracting more support from the manufacturers and therefore better salaries for the best riders, which in turn led to faster racing and so on.

This situation was fine so long as there were escalating sales to generate funds for soaring race budgets but when the slump hit the western countries, Grand Prix motocross found itself in a mammoth tangle — and one from which it has yet to extricate itself.

The reasons for the problems are not too difficult to ascertain. In 1983, the top Japanese riders were earning in excess of $500,000. In fact, Honda's racing budget for 1983 was rumoured to be £1.75 million. A credible figure when one considers that at the crucial 1983 San Marino Grand Prix — the race which effectively decided the fate of the 1983 World Championship — there were 24 Honda staff serving three Honda riders. Except for a flag flying from the turret and a sentry on the rampart, the Honda enclave at Baldasserona reminded me of nothing less than a large US cavalry fort with vans and motorhomes forming the walls. Impressive by any standards, but at what expense!

The end of the 1983 season saw several quite remarkable events take place. In contrast to the three Honda riders, Hakan Carlqvist won the 500 cc world title with the assistance of his girlfriend and Tommy, his mechanic. Suzuki pulled out altogether leaving the 250 World Champion, Georges Jobe, without a ride, whilst Honda parted company with Graham Noyce and reportedly cut Andre Malherbe's salary by 50%.

Cagiva introduced a brand-new 500 ridden by the fiery Russians, Lodovski and Kudiakov. Sometimes with doubtful success, as Lodovski waits for the rescue crew after timed training at the Swiss Grand Prix.

**Joel Robert with the 250cc Suzuki at Dodington in June 1970.**

Kawasaki continued to maintain a high profile both through an official works team headed by the likeable Laurence Spence — although the Ulsterman's salary was definitely in the "budget" bracket when compared to the golden days of motocross — and skilful a use of redundant riders from two other factories. When both Dave Watson — who rode for Yamaha — and Suzuki's Georges Jobe were left without bikes at the end of 1983, they were loosely absorbed into the Kawasaki G.P. effort, running their own teams but riding Kawasaki machines. A clever way of gaining maximum G.P. penetration for minimum cost.

By the time this book appears on sale, I feel sure that we will have seen a move, or the beginnings of a move, by all manufacturers to restrict the bikes used in all G.P. classes to production models. There is much to be said for this approach, for

any motocross machine made today is a fast, spectacular beast and in the 500 cc class, many riders consider the ordinary production machines to be too much of a good thing in every respect. Certainly, Thorpe, Carlqvist, Malherbe, Jobe and Geboers on well set-up standard bikes will produce racing just as exciting as in the present grands prix where inevitably the race will be won by a rider aboard a super special works machine.

However, motocross finance and policy, fascinating though they are, are not the main aim of this book so let us conclude this chapter by briefly examining the big leaps forward which were made in the period 1974–84.

First of these was the advent of what have become known as the "Rocketship" engines. This term was clearly American but the name of its originator has been lost with the passage of time. It's aim was clear: to identify those engines which followed the style of Heikki Mikkola's 1977 and 1978 World Championship winning bikes. These were the first of the truly big bore two-strokes with a capacity of over 450 cc and a power output in excess of 50 bhp. They left the competitive 400s — such as the Maico campaigned by Graham Noyce until he joined the Honda team — gasping for breath.

**Roger de Coster was a factory rider for CZ before joining Suzuki so successfully.**

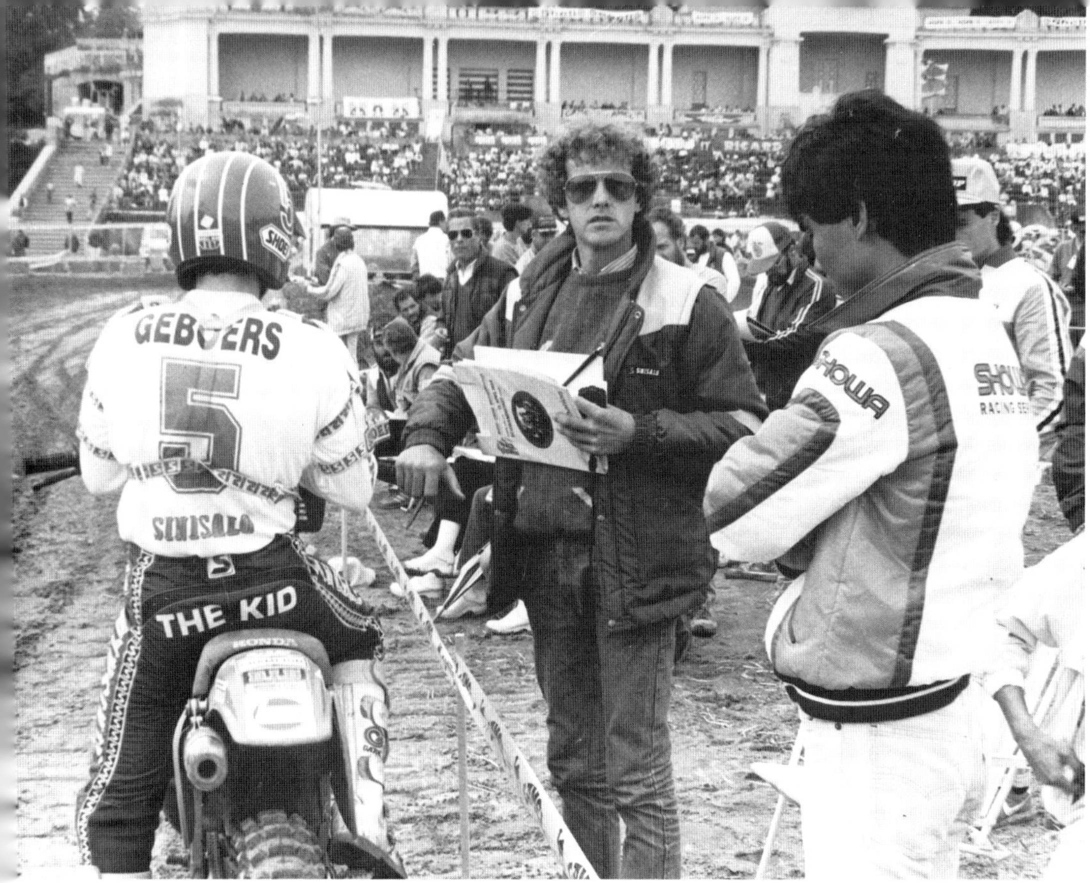

Eric Geboers.

Arch rival Heikki Mikkola flies the big Yamaha at Markelo.

How much of the big Yamaha's success is attributable to the ultra-fast motors and how much to Mikkola will always be fiercely debated. It is unquestionably true that the bikes were the fastest in the world but they were far from the best handling. In Mikkola, Yamaha had one of the fittest and most aggressive riders ever to ride motocross and as he did with the 360 Husqvarna in 1974, he showed that given the power, he could use it to dominate a race. Some of the best motocross I have ever seen provided a poignant contrast between the fluid and smooth De Coster and the violently fierce Mikkola, with neither rider having clear superiority despite their radically different styles.

In any history of motocross — even one as brief as this — one rider above all others should be mentioned. That rider is Roger de Coster. Five times World Champion, Roger won every title against the toughest opposition and often defied all the odds to succeed. As a rider, he was a delight to watch. So smooth, that he made Grand Prix motocross look ludicrously simple, the key to his speed being his relentless perfection. There was never an inch of the track which he did not ride to the limits of his abilities and yet rarely did he crash.

De Coster was also one of the most perceptive riders ever to compete in motocross. His feel for a bike was uncanny and his desire to work on, and improve, his own bike — with or without the help of his mechanic — is legendary. But for me, Roger should be remembered most for neither of these two traits, but for his humanity. He is outstandingly the most intelligent and articulate rider I have met and his ability to converse in at least three languages with total fluency gives him an access to the media which is far more wide ranging than any other World Champion has achieved before or since.

**Graham Noyce in action during the 1979 West German Grand Prix at Beuerne.**

**The sophisticated elegance of the 1984 works Honda.**

Yet, despite all these attributes, Roger is a genuinely warm, modest person. I met him in 1983 after a gap of two years, and although I am far from being an intimate acquaintance, he welcomed me, remembered my name and chatted as if we were old friends. In truth, I was probably one of two or three hundred journalists he talked to in the same period and still he could show me the same warmth and courtesy he would if we were next-door-neighbours. Roger de Coster no longer graces the tracks as a rider and the motocross world is a poorer place for that.

Whilst Yamaha and Suzuki were slogging it out in the limelight, Honda arrived on the scene and first Brad Lackey and then Graham Noyce. Lackey was in strong contention for the 1978 World Championship but switched camps to Kawasaki in 1979, the year which gave Noyce his first World Championship. This was a memorable year for Noyce, Honda and motocross. It was the last time that a championship would be won by a motorcycle using twin rear dampers controlling the swinging arm — the system which had been employed since the advent of sprung rear wheels.

Lackey arrived on the scene with rising rate rear suspension controlled by a single centrally-mounted damper. The story of this season is a fascinating one with Lackey winning more motos than any other rider but Noyce failing to finish only two races all year thanks to the impeccable work of his mechanic, Bill Buchka.

Whilst Noyce campaigned the old-fashioned but well-proven Honda, Kawasaki struggled with five different engines and almost as many frames. My heart goes out to Kawasaki since they raced a bike which was only finished three months before the first grand prix and nearly succeeded in winning a World Championship. Anyone interested in reading the whole story could do worse than read my book *The Big Leap – Ten Years of Motocross.* Kawasaki dragged the whole motocross world forward with their suspension system which was a quantum leap in chassis technology. It took everyone else a season to catch up, but now we are on a plateau in which the refinement of existing ideas is more important than seeking completely fresh approaches. Designing ways of softening the power delivery – either by altering the capacity of the expansion chamber as in the Honda ATAC system, or by variable exhaust ports as first used on the 500 cc Grand Prix Yamaha but not yet on the big production bikes – has now arrived.

Hydraulics have also made themselves known both in the use of disc brakes – an idea which has found its way on to production bikes – and also in hydraulic clutches, a system which the club rider will no doubt be pleased to live without, if the number of riders struggling with disc brakes is any guide.

Finally, watercooling has made its presence felt with the majority of marques of most capacities now liquid-cooled – again not always to the benefit of the club racer. I want to finish this chapter thinking about the ordinary lad or girl who is racing, for this book, as I have said, is theirs.

Yes, the G.P.s, the works stars and the factory exotica are all interesting but this book is about motocross for the ordinary rider who isn't going to win a World Championship but who wants to enjoy racing, whether he finishes first or last. Winning at any level is great but if you can finish second, third or last and **ENJOY** yourself, then you have really found the secret of motocross.

*Facing page:*
**1979 West German 500 GP, Benene Lackey frolicked during practice, but not during the race!**

# Clothing

IN 1969, the height of fashion 'and the state of the art in design' were leather motocross jeans — black, naturally, — with padded knees and a double yellow stripe down the leg. Two thin stripes were considered very *avante garde* and suitable for young, dilettante riders who did not mind strutting around like peacocks. I know, I was one myself! Now it seems that nothing is too daring, or radical, to raise an eyebrow amongst even the most conservative of riders. Certainly, multi-coloured everything is *de rigeur* today.

However, not only has clothing become more brightly coloured but it is infinitely more practical, offering much greater protection and durability than in the days of yore. Of course, every rider wants to look smart and fashionable at races, but do bear in mind that the primary task of motocross clothing is to provide protection. It is no use at all looking smart and then paying the penalty for your sartorial elegance in hospital.

Equally, remember that all top riders will receive their clothing free and in many cases they will be paid for using the equipment. Naturally, they will be doing all they can to persuade you to buy the items they are contracted to promote. This being the case, the fact that rider Zaphod Beeblebrox happens to be Atlantean motocross champion does not automatically mean that his riding apparel is the best buy. By all means, look what the top riders are wearing and then make your own decisions on price and quality.

The same must be said of the items I have illustrated in this chapter. For example, I am sponsored by Arai Helmets and Clover Clothing. I personally believe that every article I have included is at least as good as the best on sale at present but I am not saying that only Arai and Clover make good products: rather, that these are the standards at which to aim. If you can find an equally good item — or a better one — at a more attractive price, then buy it.

We will examine the riding gear in order of importance since some aspects of a rider's clothing are critically important and others less so. First, the helmet.

As I have noted, my first choice is an Arai, Why? The most important reason is that the helmet comes from a well-known, reputable company. Take a chance on some one-off jeans from a back-street company if you must, but not with a helmet. It is essential to have a well-known product with a proven reputation.

Arai helmets are made of glass-fibre and this material is still my own preference for a helmet shell. It is a difficult, time-consuming method of manufacture to adopt, but it has a number of benefits for the motocross rider. First, it is tolerant of scratches and chips. Second, it is unaffected by petrol or solvents such as contact cleaner — although please do not try to clean your helmet with a chemical solvent. Third, it can be resprayed at the end of the season — thus extending its life considerably.

Finally, a good glass-fibre helmet should meet the three most stringent safety standards applicable to motocross. These are the BS: 2495 — 77 amendment 5; the American Snell '80 and finally the ACU Gold Label. Of these three, the BSI mark is the most important, although the ACU label is beginning to carry some real weight now that this organisation has begun failing helmets rather than accepting everything which was offered.

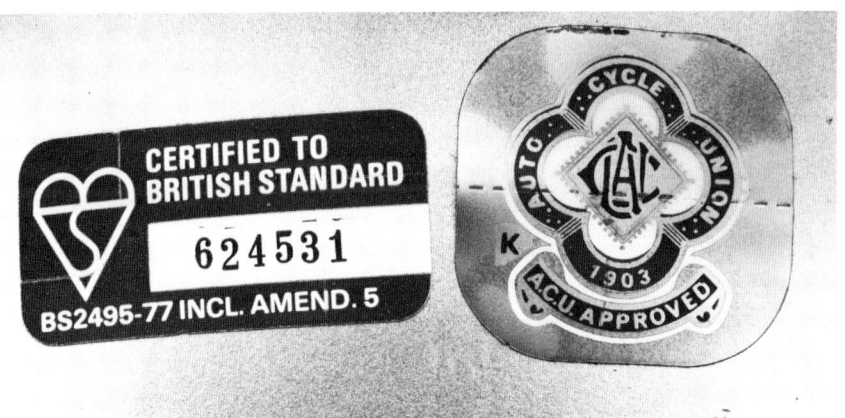

**A helmet must have the ACU 'gold' sticker and the accompanying British Standards certification to BS2495 if used in motocross competition events.**

Any helmet you consider must meet at least BS: 2495 and the ACU Gold Label. The Snell is a good standard but rather political in its application, making it difficult for a thermoplastic helmet to reach the required standards.

An equally firm rule is that any helmet chosen must be full-face. This can take the form of an integral part of the helmet like a Bell or an MDS or an adjustable face guard such as the Arai. Motocross is simply too fast now for the old-fashioned type of clip-on face guard which will do absolutely nothing for the rider in the case of an accident and provides scant protection against flying debris either.

There are disadvantages with a glass fibre helmet and the most critical of these is cost. Laying down a good shell by hand is difficult and therefore expensive. Glass-fibre helmets are also heavier than thermoplastic designs — unless one pays

a lot of money for the very best, which can be made as light as any other material. It is much easier to get a good helmet with a thermoplastic shell which will be injection moulded, using polycarbonate. Quality can be assured by having first-class manufacturing equipment and meticulous quality control. Again, this points to a known manufacturer with a sound reputation.

Polycarbonate must not be painted under any circumstances and although this material is now much more resistant to degradation by petrol, a question mark still hangs over it in this respect. Keep thermoplastics away from contact cleaner at all costs!

The fit of the helmet is very important and it cannot be stressed too highly that it should be on the tight side of snug. The reason for this is rather macabre but must be understood for the rider's own safety. Inside the shell is a polystyrene liner which is the part of the helmet which actually absorbs the shock of an accident. Between the rider's head and the liner is a layer of soft foam which acts as a sizing band. In a severe accident, the rider's head accelerates into the liner and is then braked sharply. The brain membrane is torn away and the brain hits the skull. The greater the distance the head has to accelerate then the higher the risk of this happening. If the head has only a few millimetres to accelerate before it is stopped by the liner, then the helmet has the greatest possible chance of absorbing the energy created by the impact in the first milli-seconds after it has happened — the only period when the rider is in any real danger.

A secondary benefit of having a firm-fitting helmet is that it will not waggle about on the rider's head during a race. Having one's vision obscured after landing on a big jump is, to say the least, disconcerting.

Of almost equal importance to the helmet are the goggles. At first, riding with goggles is difficult and even an uncomfortable experience but do persevere. I will now not ride for any reason — racing or practice — without wearing goggles and I am now scarcely aware of their presence.

**Scott goggles with stacked tear-offs.**

Like the helmet, choose a reputable model which has been expressly designed for motocross use. The frame should be wide and comfortable with a broad strap which will not slip on the helmet. Try to ascertain whether or not the lens is scratch-resistant polycarbonate. This is the material used for visors on full-face road helmets and it is worth paying the extra for it since it is much more abrasion resistant than ordinary polycarbonate. My own choice is Scott, which satisfies all these criteria and represents the state of the art at the time of writing.

The goggles should have some method of attaching tear-offs. These are very thin plastic covers which are fitted to the front of the actual lens. They can be stacked on top of one another and when one layer is dirty it is removed with one hand, revealing a clean one underneath. As many as five tear-offs can be stacked on top of each other, permitting goggles to be worn throughout muddy races.

The latest innovation in tear-off technology is the Smith roll-off system which provides the equivalent of dozens of tear-offs in a long, thin film rather like a 35mm film cassette. This is the neatest solution to the problem so far and works very well on the right day. Unfortunately, the mechanism jams in very wet or sandy conditions but if you can afford the high cost, roll-offs are worth considering for whatever make of goggle you use.

Next in line of priority is the boots. At one time, it seemed plastic boots would provide the answer to every racer's dream but experience has shown that the best synthetic materials cannot match good cowhide for flexibility, durability and

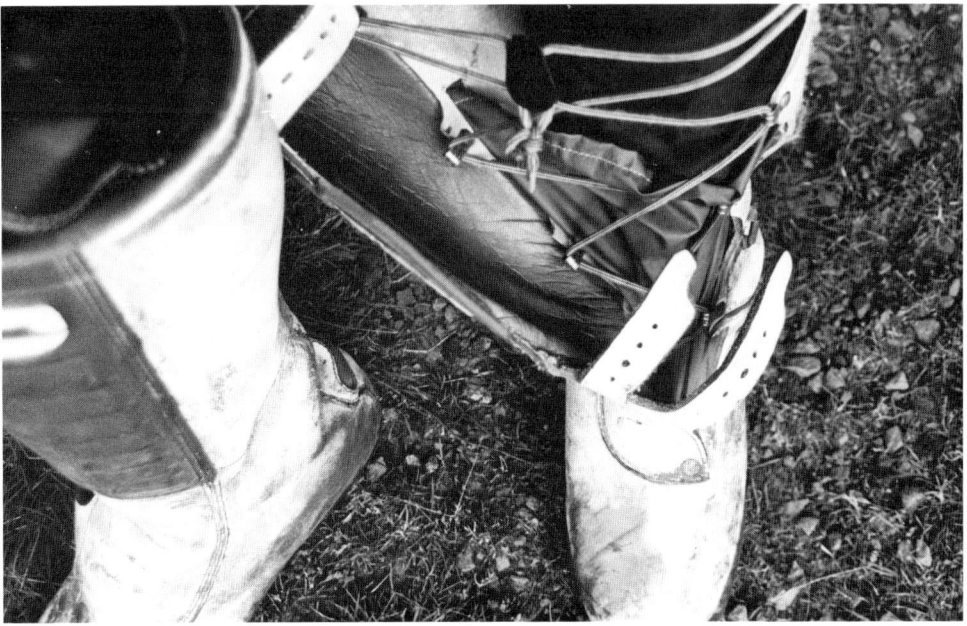

**Drawstrings on a boot are a big safety factor. Always wear the boot as tight as possible.**

strength. Like a helmet, a boot should be firm-fitting and should always be strapped up tight. On the Clover design, an internal drawstring pulls the boot tight on to the rider's leg. This is a worthwhile feature and also has the additional benefit of making it easy to strap them up to the necessary degree of tightness.

For 1984, a number of manufacturers introduced a barred sole, replacing the long-established slipper pattern. For many years, riders enjoyed the benefits of a slipper sole which allowed the boot to skate over ground without snagging. Unfortunately, the smooth sole meant that walking in the paddock on a muddy wet day was hazardous and pushing a bike, impossible. The new style floats over rough terrain just as well as ever but the bars mean that traction is available for walking.

Make sure that the boot you choose does have really substantial protection for the shin. On the Clover boot, this is provided by a thick layer of polythene, backed by solid foam rubber. This should be the minimum acceptable in any boot. All good boots are now very expensive. In order to preserve their life as long as possible, it is worth noting some simple tips for boot care.

First, never force-dry boots in front of a radiator or fire. This can cause internal burning of the leather which will dramatically reduce their life. It is far better to let them dry naturally in the workshop — keeping them well-aired to avoid the chances of mould growth.

After every outing the boots should be lubricated, but I would not advise using dubbin. This makes the leather too soft and will reduce the protection the boot offers. Instead, use ordinary shoe polish, or hide food, every week and a coat of dubbin once a month. Treated in this way, boots will have a sensible working life.

**The new type of barred sole is the only one to use now.**

Perhaps the biggest step forward that has been made in motocross protection in the last ten years is in body armour. The early body armour was heavy, uncomfortable and none too effective — although it was a 100% improvement on nothing! Now there are many good designs on the market although in my opinion, none that is perfect or even as good as is capable of being made. My own body armour is made from two sets — the front an M. Robert design and the back taken from a Motocross Fox unit. The reason I went to all this trouble is that the M. Robert design, whilst giving excellent protection to the front and shoulders of the rider, left the spine and back exposed. Clearly this was unsatisfactory.

**Apico's anatomic leg guards are a big step forward.**

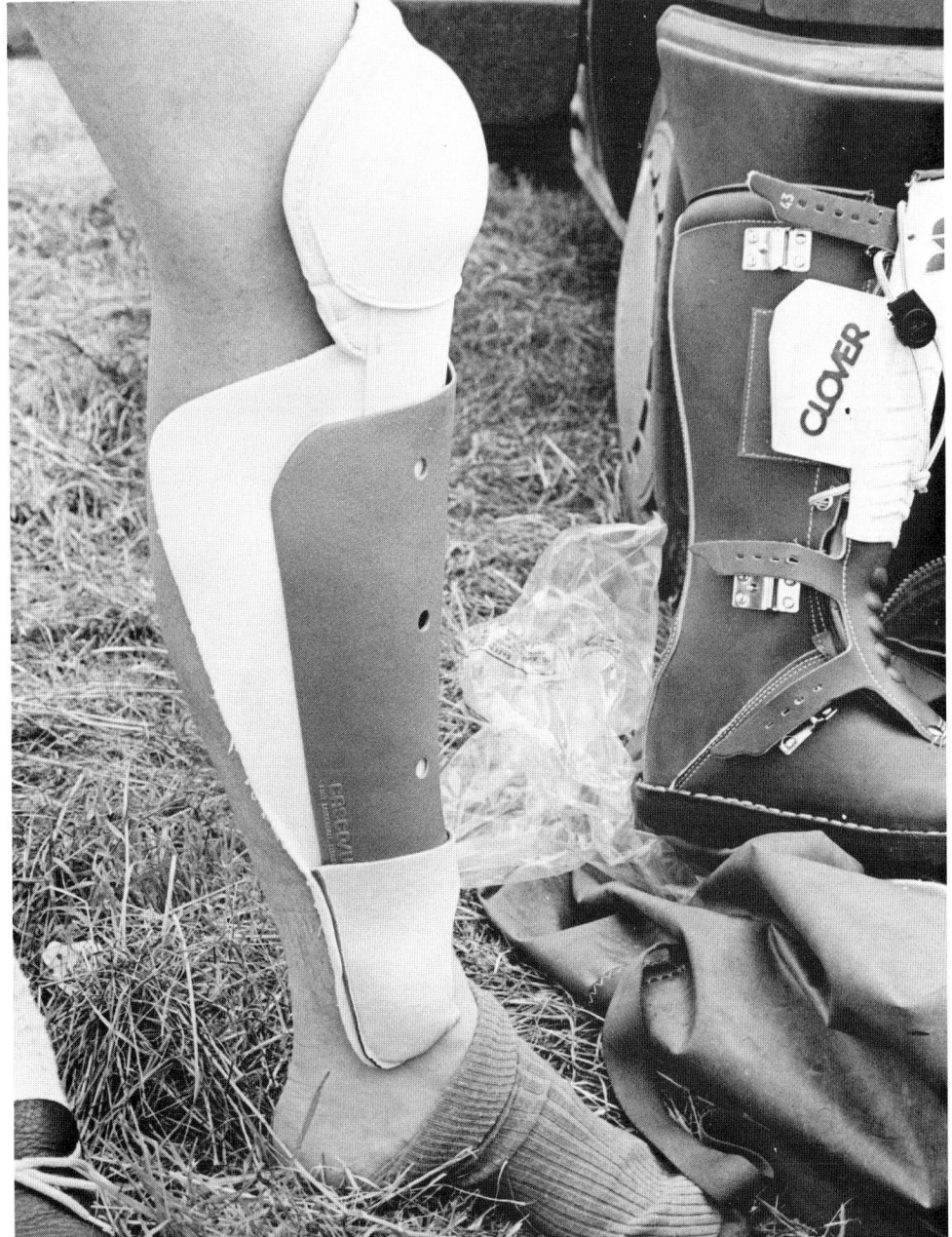

Of the standard items, the UFO Plast is as good as any in offering a good degree of protection and overlap between segments. This overlap is vital for much of the value of body armour comes from its ability to deflect the impact. This is done by one piece of the armour sliding and twisting over the other, thus changing the angle of impact from at or near 90° to a more oblique blow. The shallower the angle, the less chance there will be of injury.

Another interesting development is the British Pro-Tech body armour which has a very dense shock-absorbing foam, rather like the liner on a helmet. A criticism which is made of high density polythene armour is that it is such a solid material that it will in fact transmit shock to a rider's body just like a centre-punch hit by a hammer. The Pro-Tech answers this problem but falls prey to another. The foam itself is too soft to prevent penetration by a sharp object, for example a rock or the end of a handlebar. In this respect, the solid armour is far superior. Ideally, one would need a Pro-Tech absorbent foam with a thin layer of hard plastic covering it. This would be full body armour with very similar characteristics to a helmet.

**The author's own composite body armour, the best alternative to the lack of wholly satisfactory protection available at the time of writing.**

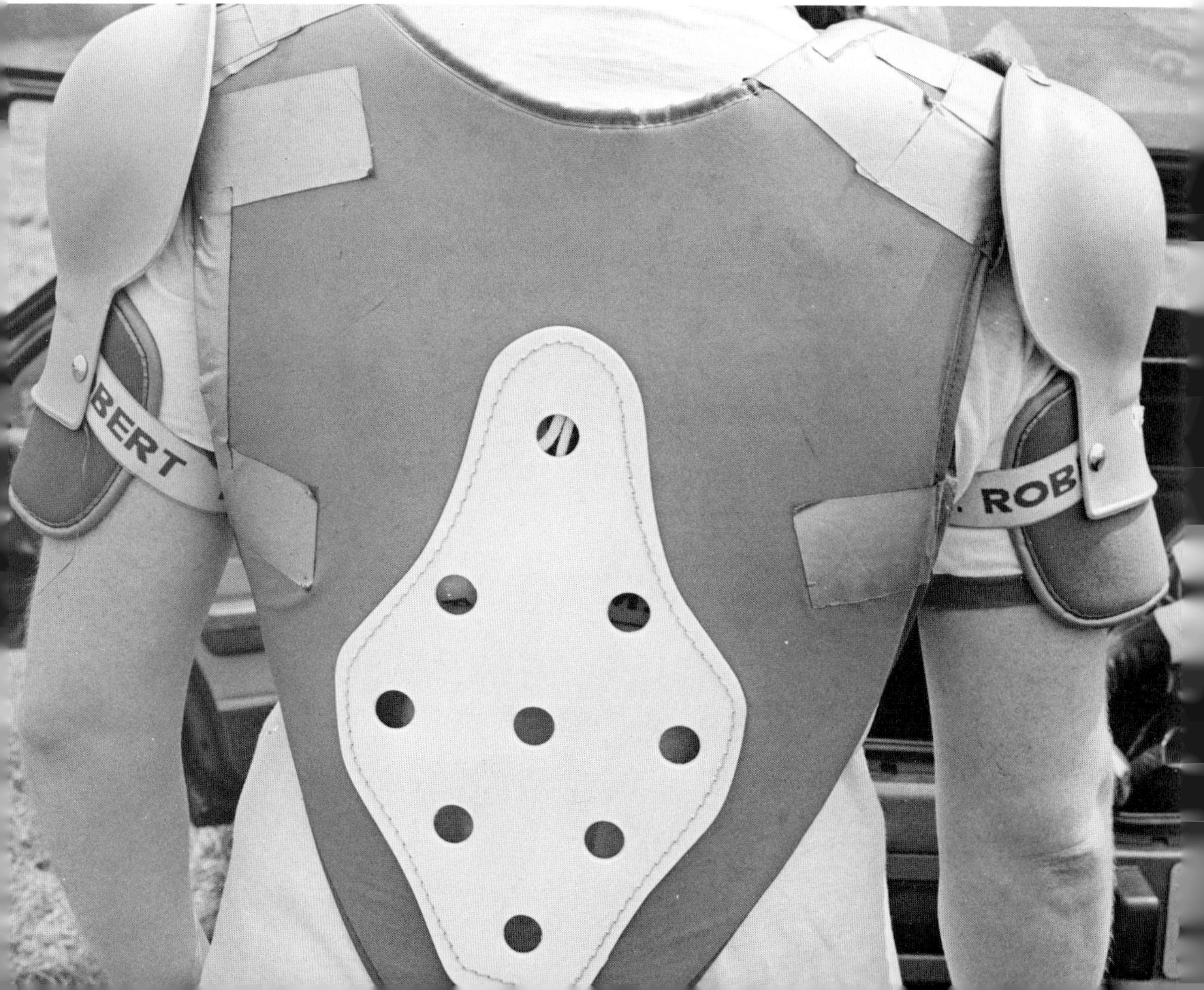

As well as covering the shoulders, chest and back, there are now protectors made for the elbows and lower legs. These seem to be a most sensible step forward and should be considered as essential as the rest of the rider's protective gear.

Even allowing for the present inadequacies of body armour, do wear the best available. My most serious accident in 18 years racing was caused by being flicked off a bike at 5 mph and hitting a sharp rock at 90°. The impact broke my shoulder and could have been completely avoided by body armour of any kind. Learn from my mistake!

One point to note is that many riders opt to wear a T-shirt beneath their body armour. This prevents chafing which can be painful as the armour skids up and down a naked body. Any rider who has had his nipples abraded by body armour soon becomes a T-shirt fan.

All motocross jeans are now made in nylon with the best ones having leather seats for comfort. Leather jeans are not only prohibitively expensive but they are also hotter, heavier and infinitely less hygenic than modern jeans, which can be thrown in the washing machine along with the rest of the riding gear. Good features to look for are elasticated legs which will stop rucks forming underneath one's boots. These can leave painful weals when the boots are tightened up firmly. Like the boots, look for good protection for the knee and shin. In this respect, it is vital to have absorbent foam since a layer of stiff plastic which is unable to twist and therefore deflect shock will transmit it beautifully and broken bones may result.

Again, the ideal solution is to have a knee cap which has an outer layer of hard plastic with a softer liner. This system will protect both the rider and liner from injury from sharp objects and is available in the best jeans. My own choice is a combination of the Clover jeans — which are beautifully designed and very comfortable — and the Apico anatomic leg guard which gives the maximum protection.

There are very many cheap jeans on sale and perhaps some riders will be forced by budgetary considerations to go for the minimum cost. However, do think carefully. I have seen cheap Taiwanese jeans ripped apart after three meetings whilst a good pair of jeans will last ten or twenty times longer. The Clover jeans pictured are particularly good in this respect.

Gloves are like body armour — they are a long way off being perfect, or even satisfactory. At present, they do not offer sufficient protection and one can only cast envious eyes at the quality of cricketing gloves. Try to get the best finger protection offered so that at least some of the flying stones are deflected and look for gloves which do not bunch when the handlebar is gripped. Also, consider the problem of cheap gloves wearing out very rapidly and the false economy this represents.

My Clover gloves are very near to the "state of the art". Some riders would argue they are the best and they feature not only extremely dense foam to protect the rider's fingers but also curved palms and ventilated strips at the sides to keep the palms as cool as possible. There is a very marked difference between specialist gloves such as these and cheap Asian imitations, and it is worth considering the savings involved compared with the extra comfort and also longevity of top quality items. Although something of a luxury, Clover also make wet weather gloves with synthetic palms made from a material not unlike that used for cleaning windows. These do give a much better grip and if your budget can run to two pairs of gloves they are a worthwhile buy.

A good racing glove should have curved palms to reduce blistering. This Clover glove has a palm made from a synthetic, rather than leather, material, which gives improved grip in muddy conditions – a good buy if you can afford two pairs of gloves.

*Facing page:* Amateur racers can't afford to buy cheap, poor quality jeans. State-of-the-art jeans, like these from Clover, will last a whole season and be more comfortable as well.

This brings me to the centre of the rider – his stomach and marriage tackle, both vital in their respective ways. Personally I have never found the need for special supportive briefs – perhaps I am not sufficiently well-endowed – and I would suggest that cotton briefs courtesy of Marks and Spencer do the job as well

**Points worth noting in this serious racing glove are the dense padding for good finger protection, the debris-proof wrist band, and the ventilated side strips.**

as anything. They also have the additional benefit of being comfortable for a whole day, an important factor if one considers that scrutineering will be at 9 am and the last race may not be until 6.30 pm.

A body belt is worth wearing not only for the assistance it gives to the stomach muscles but also as added protection for the kidneys. As with all the other items we have considered, go for a well-known brand that is in use for racing rather than trying to misappropriate big sister's foundation garment.

Finally, to a vital part of the rider's equipment – his race shirt. Although I would freely acknowledge that I am sponsored by Clover and therefore biased towards that company's product, their silky race shirts really are my favourite to wear. They are cool and comfortable and last forever. Yet, in this book you will not see me wearing one. Why? The answer quite simply lies in sponsorship. Given complete freedom of choice, I would wear a Clover shirt but if other contracts clash – such as my responsibilities towards Crooks-Suzuki, Rock Oil or Dunlop – then I must wear a shirt which meets with these requirements.

Certainly, it is very pleasant to race in a top-quality race shirt but the facts of the matter are that the shirt is not vital to the rider's comfort nor his safety. It is not worth inflicting injury on one's wallet for the sake of having a more pleasant shirt. If you have to buy a shirt, go for a top quality item like the Clover satin design but preferably, try to get a shirt for free. Many professional riders have begun their careers with nothing more than free shirts and certainly the skills learnt in scrounging shirts can be of great value later.

To conclude this chapter, it is worth mentioning wet weather gear. This may be divided into two categories. Practice gear, which can be waterproof and keep the rider dry and clean, and race gear. The jacket or oversuit suitable for practising will unfortunately be too bulky to race in, so for the latter, a very thin nylon jacket and overtrousers should suffice. I have a horrible cheap Italian race jacket and a pair of overtrousers which are totally non-waterproof but are ideal for resisting mud.

For cold weather, and for practising in winter, I have a Clover enduro jacket which is warm and dry and very comfortable but is rather bulky for motocross. Again, a good quality enduro jacket is worth the investment if your budget allows since it will last for years and also doubles as excellent paddock wear. But if your budget is limited, perhaps this is one item which can wait.

To conclude, choose gear which is safe first and fashionable second. Do consider the quality of the design and think carefully about the false economies which can result from buying cheap equipment and which will wear out instantly. Any item which cannot last a whole season – damage caused by major crashes excepted – should not be found in the budget racer's wardrobe. Only the sponsored stars can afford the luxury of cheap and nasty gear.

# Buying a bike

BUYING a racing bike can be as exciting as winning one's first race or as disappointing as having your ex-girl-friend arrive at a meeting with your best mate —the height of ecstasy or the depths of despair. However, with some forethought and a little patience, it is possible to ensure that the exercise is not only painless —except for the essential expenditure — but also an enjoyable experience! Your cunning and knowledge might also impress future girl-friends too!

The first decision to be made is the choice of engine capacity. In schoolboy racing, the capacity class is largely determined by the age of the rider, but once a racer is old enough to compete independently, he may opt for two-stroke bikes of 125 cc, 250 cc, 500 cc or a four-stroke (usually raced in a class of its own and invariably of a large capacity — often over 600 cc). Of these four choices, there is only one viable option for the newcomer — the 250. To understand why this is so clearly the best choice, let us consider the merits and drawbacks of the alternatives.

First, the 125 cc class. These bikes are extremely fast — in many cases setting lap times quicker than bigger bikes. However, they do need to be ridden very hard. All the power from little bikes is produced at the very top of the power band and this means that they must be revved continuously. When used correctly, they are great fun and, as we have noted, competitive with anything. But keeping a little bike buzzing is not an easy task for a beginner — particularly one who is learning riding and racing techniques at the same time.

Maintenance too, is demanding, since the very high revs of these bikes exact a high toll in terms of engine wear. Most 125 owners will soon be replacing items such as pistons, reed petals and even cylinder barrels as a matter of routine. Therefore, on the dual counts of running costs and riding difficulty, avoid the

**If you are as good at judging bikes as Bill Brown, you might just end up with a bike like his — and a 'Roller' to go with it.**

125 cc — unless of course you happen to have had experience of these bikes as a schoolboy and have particularly enjoyed riding them or are of very slight stature and would benefit from their lightness.

At the other end of the scale are the 500s. Quite simply, these are too much of a good thing in every respect. Any modern 500 is frighteningly fast and not just so for the novice either! There are precious few experts who can ride this class

satisfactorily. Strangely, wear is not a problem with big bikes for the simple reason that so few riders are capable of working them really hard.

The main danger for the novice is that a 500 develops bad riding habits and discourages mastery of good ones. Once a 500 is on the move, changing gear is almost an irrelevance since there is so much power that the bike will scorch along merely by opening the throttle. This in turn leads to a lazy riding technique where the rider becomes obsessed with the idea of squirting the power on the straights and not making a full effort on the corners.

The other difficulty is that a 500 can often be a law unto itself in the hands of the less-than-expert rider. Careless use of the throttle on jumps, cambered surfaces or climbs can lead to all sorts of tangles that the novice can well do without, so avoid these bikes unless there are mitigating circumstances. These may be identified in two areas. First, if the rider is a big, burly lad it may be that a 500 is about right for dragging large lumps of body about. Second, using the guidelines we will discuss later, it could be that the buy of the century is to be had in a second-hand bike.

Should your heart be set on a 500, then do buy a bike that has a reputation for being easy to ride. It is a straightforward job to tune almost any 500 cc motocross engine so that it produces 60 bhp. What is far more difficult is making that power useable.

The same rules we have identified with the 500 cc two-strokes can be applied to the four-stroke class — only more so. I love this class but it is really so far removed from mainstream motocross that the newcomer will learn only specialised 'banger' habits which are difficult to transfer to other classes.

Also, beware of myths about four-stroke reliability. A modern four-stroke **WILL** last very well — if it is cared for. Should it not be, a small mortgage will have to be raised to rebuild it. The chassis too, is very maintenance sensitive. These beasts are big, heavy and hard on the frame, forks and wheels. Better by far to learn one's craft on a less demanding creature: the 250 cc two-stroke. I must confess to a personal bias towards this class, for having ridden everything from a 50 cc Fantic to 980 cc BMWs — all off-road racers too — I return to the 250 as the most pleasant of all the capacities.

The reasons for my affection is that the quarter litre bikes have all the virtues which the other classes offer and few of their vices. To be fair, they do no single thing as well as a 125 or a 500 since they are in effect a compromise. However, they are near-perfect tools on which to learn the craft of motocross, for above all else, they are fun bikes to ride.

What a beginner needs is a motorcycle which will teach him the basic motocross techniques which can be later perfected as experience is gained. The bike should also be enjoyable and forgiving to ride. Thus, a 250 can be revved like a 125 or powered out of a corner like a 500. It is light enough to give an easy ride and sufficiently heavy to demand the correct positioning of body-weight if the bike is to perform at its best. Best of all, 250s seem exceptionally sturdy and long-lasting bikes which will make no more demands on the rider's mechanical skill and time than the minimum necessary to keep any competition bike in satisfactory condition.

Finally, all racing motorcycles need to be worked hard if they are to perform properly. Burbling round on pilot jet will make even the most exciting bike seem dull. The novice has more chance of getting a 250 into its stride than any other class. For this reason alone, go for the midweight bikes.

**An easy-to-ride 250 is by far the best choice for a beginner. It is the best fun to ride of any capacity.**

The next question which must be answered comes in two parts. First, do I buy a new bike or second-hand? Second, shall I buy the bike privately or through a dealer? Both these elements are of vital importance.

Let us consider the question of new or second-hand. There is a school of thought which might be identified as the "ride-a-wreck-because-you-won't-know-any-better-to-begin-with" philosophy. Frankly, I feel this argument is fallacious if only because the beginner with a real interest in motocross soon becomes knowledgeable and equally quickly, becomes aware of the shortcomings of his bike. Wrecks are just traps for the unwary which will gobble up money quicker than you can earn overtime or scrounge from your Mum. Stay away from cheap bikes even if they are given to you free.

Now, to the wider question of second-hand bikes. These can be the best buy for most riders and shortly, we will discuss the ground rules for buying a used machine. The key factor in buying a bike is to know where it came from.

Take my own bike for example. I am no longer competitive so I don't ride it hard but I am very experienced so I use the machine skilfully. My maintenance is first class — almost to the point of fanaticism — and so buying one of my bikes would

**The author's immaculate 250 Crooks-Suzuki. A bike like this is always worth buying second-hand.**

present a sound investment since the depreciation on any new motorcycle is horrific. The converse situation would apply to a machine belonging to a young rider, with a lot of courage but not much skill and lacking in mechanical experience. His motorcycle should be avoided like the plague.

At present, with many new motorcycles costing nearer £2000 than £1750, I do not feel that the investment needed to purchase an unused bike is justifiable for riders at less than expert level. Yes, you might gain an extra two or three places but if you are riding for fun, then remember that the cost of those extra places is the difference between a new and second-hand bike: in cash terms, probably £800 or £900! Is each improvement in place really worth £300?

The exception to this rule is to buy a brand-new twelve months old bike. If this sounds confusing it is worth remembering that each year, most manufacturers overproduce and have a stock of machines which were unsold in that current model year. As bikes develop, the year-old ones lose their attraction for the most demanding riders and so have to be sold off at a heavy discount. These bikes are the most desirable of all since they have all the advantages of reliability and crispness which only a new bike can give whilst requiring no more financial outlay than a good second-hand machine.

Unfortunately, the manufacturers have begun to realise that over-production is not only financially damaging in terms of loss of revenue caused by the discount price but also that potential buyers of new machines will often prefer to buy a twelve month old bike — probably of very similar specification — at a substantial saving. And quite right too. Any rider who does not need the ultimate in performance would be silly if he did not do the same thing.

This brings us to the second part of the question: to buy privately or from the trade? Anyone considering buying a bike privately would do well to learn by heart the adage, *Caveat Emptor* – let the buyer beware. Remember, if you buy a bike from another rider there will be no guarantee with it, nor will the vendor, ( if he has a grain of commonsense) give any assurance about the future performance of the machine. All that he can or will say is that the bike is here, look at it and make your own judgement.

This Maico was second-hand and although almost better than new, was £700 cheaper. This is the sort of bike which makes a very good buy – particularly when backed by the after-sales service of a reputable dealer.

If you are uneasy about being able to assess a racing bike competently, you should not even consider a private purchase. Buying a bike from the trade has two distinct advantages for the novice. For example, take a bike bought from a dealer on his recommendation that it is a sound machine for a beginner. Perhaps the previous owner was known personally to him. Now, say a rear damper rod breaks

at the first outing, (and this sort of thing does happen in real life). The dealer is under no legal obligation to do anything because the damper rod was sound whilst the machine was in his shop and therefore the bike was fit for sale. However, morally he will be under strong pressure to help you. He might rebuild the damper free of charge on an expensive bike or just invoice you for the bits and not the labour if the selling price was modest.

As always, the sensible approach is to be courteous and friendly since this will invariably result in an action by the dealer in excess of the minimum required by law. Furthermore, having bought a bike from a dealer, you are in a stronger position to come to some arrangement regarding other equipment you might need. For example, if you are spending £800 or £900, it is always worth trying to negotiate some discount on a pair of jeans or a helmet.

If you do buy privately, remember all second-hand competition bikes are worn, even one of my bikes. It will be a saint who will point out the motorcycle's faults and since there are very few saints in motorcycling you **MUST** take someone with you who can help you to assess its merits. With the help of an experienced and skilful friend — someone preferably who has previously bought second-hand competition bikes with success — some excellent buys can be had, but if you are flying solo, then go to the trade.

We will examine now the criteria for buying a second-hand bike, whether privately or from the trade. Some of the items are commonsense — though often overlooked — whilst others require a little bit of thought. Remember, **TAKE YOUR TIME**. It is the easiest task in the world to spend money. Correcting an error later can be infinitely more difficult. For help in compiling this checklist, I went to Bill Brown, who owns the world-renowned Bill Brown Motorcycles in Whitehaven, Cumbria. He probably sells more motocross bikes than anyone else in Britain and buys literally hundreds of second-hand bikes each year. As a rider himself, he is one of the caring dealers who we identified. In fact, he takes great pleasure in getting the novice off to a good start.

**Buying a bike privately means you are entirely on your own.**

## Checklist for buying a second-hand motocross bike

1. Know the reputation of the bike which you are considering. Ask around amongst your friends. Approach riders at meetings who own a bike similar to the one you are considering purchasing. Look for tests in the magazines – although these are likely to be the least helpful. Find out, for example, whether there is an acknowledged clutch problem or if the rear damper is suspect or if the bike is considered too difficult to ride or too slow to be competitive.

2. Now we come to the most critical part of assessing a bike. Have a look at the bike and see what it tells you about the previous owner. Is it neat and tidy? Are the control cables frayed? Are there any obvious signs of bodging? Conversely, are there obvious signs of care and attention having been lavished on the machine? For example, have there been sensible attempts to improve the bike? Such modifications might include a non-standard air-box, a front disc shroud or mudguard extensions. Not that any one of these items is particularly valuable in itself but rather they are indications that someone loved the bike, and looked after it.

*Above:* **A split throttle indicates a lazy and careless rider – and one deficient in the brain department since the throttle could have stuck open and killed him!**

*Right:* **This exhaust pipe has been bodged with cheap matt black paint and an ineffective heat guard. This sort of 'mod' tells you a lot about the previous owner.**

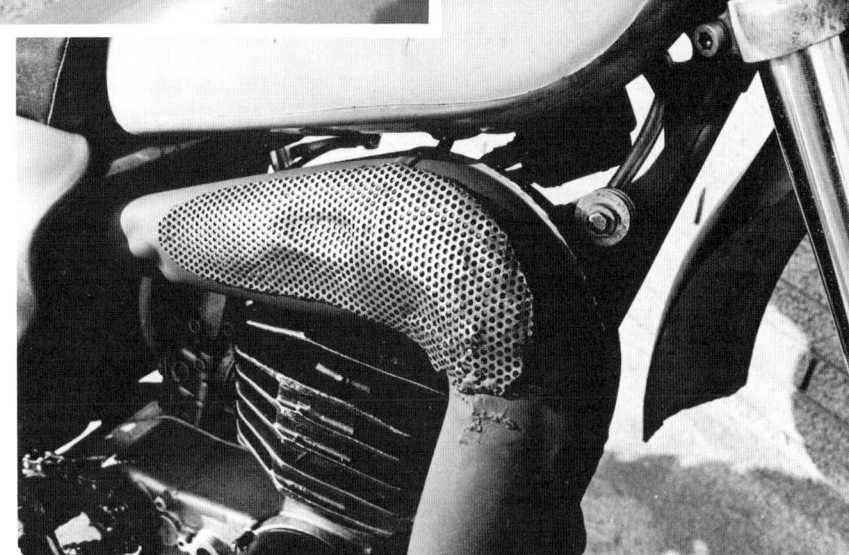

3. Now, let us begin a mechanical check. There is no one perfect way of doing this but I always begin at the front of the bike and work back. In this way, there is less likelihood of missing an important item. First, the tyres. Look at both the front and rear tyres and remember that if they are worn, the replacement costs are high. Also make sure that they are of a well-known brand and type.

4. Check the wheels. Most motocross wheels will be out of true and this is quite acceptable. What we are looking for are great big flats on the rims which will make them unsafe. If a flat is discovered, there is a good chance that there will be a crack too. A cracked rim will be fatal if it breaks at the wrong time.

5. Whilst examining the rims, check the wheel bearings for wear. Do this by turning the front wheel on to full lock — either direction will do — and then try to rock the wheel a little further. If it moves, the wheel bearing is badly worn.

6. Now spin the wheel and listen to see if the disc catches on the pads. If there is an "on-off" clicking sound, the disc may well be bent. Check this carefully. New discs are expensive.
In the case of a drum brake, spin the wheel and see if the drum makes a similar noise — indicating that it is catching on the leading brake shoe. Slacken off the adjustment so that the brake shoe no longer rubs yet is still functional when applied at the handlebar. If the brake has to be slackened off a long way at the adjuster — say six turns — before it will clear, then the hub has been distorted and is now oval. This is usually caused by careless tightening of the spokes and can lead to a cracked hub — an expensive problem to rectify.

7. Have a look at the angle of brake arm for an indication of brake shoe wear. If the arm is at 90°, or beyond it, when fully applied, then the shoes are worn out. Again, this is not a major problem but rather a bargaining point. The disc brake pads can be examined visually without removing the wheel.

8. Repeat 3, 4, 5, 6 and 7 when the rear wheel is reached.

9. On to the front forks. First, are the stanchions pitted? (these are the chrome plated legs which do not move up and down). If they are, they will be useless and very expensive to replace.

10. Are there signs of oil leaks on the stanchions? Bounce the bike up and down three or four times and then look for an oil weep around the stanchions. This means that the seals are worn. Again, not a big job but an added cost before the bike can be raced.

11. What is the feel of the fork action as it moves? If there is any hint of roughness, then look for bent stanchions and knock £150 off the price of the bike straight away. Also bent forks should ring the warning bells to look for other damage on the frame. If a rider has crashed hard enough to bend the forks, then what has he done to the rest of the bike? Find out.

12. Finally, at this stage, check the steering head bearings. Remove the weight from the front wheel and then pull the forks towards you and then push them away in an arc from about five o'clock towards three o'clock and then from five

*Facing page:* **Fork stanchions are pitted, which means the forks are effectively useless. Big money is needed to repair them.**

*Right:* Checking steering head bearings for wear.

*Below left:* Checking the swinging arm bushes for wear.

*Below right:* Oil leak on the rear damper indicates a serious problem and a previous owner who either didn't care about the bike's handling or didn't know any better. Both states are unforgivable!

to six o'clock. There should be no movement whatsoever at the steering head. When the bars are moved through their range, the movement should be smooth. If it isn't, someone devious sproat has tightened up the steering head bearing adjustment to remove the outward signs of wear even though this is easily detected by rough movement felt through the 'bars.

13. Whilst we are checking bearings, go to the swinging-arm and have a look since there is a lot of wear potential in rising-rate rear suspensions. The first thing to ascertain is whether the swinging-arm bearings are worn. Grasp the swinging-arm firmly and then try to rock it back and forth horizontally. There should be no movement at all. If there is, then the swinging-arm bearings are worn and need replacing. This is not so much an expensive job as a messy one and is a definite bargaining point.

All motocross machines now in production have single shock, rising rate rear suspension systems. By their very nature, this means that they have some form of linkage between the shock and the swinging-arm and on every pivot point is a bearing which takes incredible punishment.

It is absolutely essential that these bearings are kept well greased and there should be evidence of fresh, clean grease being applied. If they look dry and

rusty, beware. Now, with the bike supported on a stand and the rear wheel clear of the ground, gently lift the rear wheel upwards. There will almost certainly be a tiny bit of free play discernible but there shouldn't be a lot of slack. If there is enough movement to make a clear clicking noise, then the rear suspension is worn and probably a complete set of bearings will be needed. This is not a cheap job. Having said this, if they are well maintained, these rising rate suspensions last a long time which reiterates the point about making sure that your second-hand bike came from a good home.

14. Now, politely ask the owner to remove the tank and seat. This is not really more than a two minute job and he shouldn't mind. Look for cracks around the steering head on the frame and also around the bottom engine rails – where the bike might have hit a rock – and the engine mountings. Also, if the bike is water-cooled, check for damage to the radiator whilst the tank is off and the radiator can be examined from all sides. Check for water leaks on the hoses at the same time. Hoses are cheap to replace but a new radiator requires a bank loan.

15. Now to the engine. The bike should start easily on the kick start. Having said this, some bikes are reluctant to fire up from cold but if the owner, who knows the beast intimately, can't persuade the thing to run in under a couple of minutes, then you will stand no chance. Does the bike sound crisp and healthy? Before starting the bike-buying process, listen to some good bikes at meetings and try to remember their sound. Your bike should sound similar. If it coughs and bangs and produces clouds of blue smoke, quickly recall an important engagement elsewhere and leave.

Ideally, you should have a short ride on the bike – even twenty yards up and down a grass verge is sufficient to check that all the advertised gears are present and correct and that the clutch is functioning properly. If this is impossible, find all the gears with the engine stopped.

If you are very lucky, you might even get a proper test ride on a track. Should this happen, do remember the old adage, " benders, menders". Try to impress the present owner with your skill and crash his bike in the process and you will be honour-bound to buy it or pay for the repairs. Just have a quiet play on the machine and ascertain that everything is working smoothly.

16. Back to visual checks. Look at the water-pump for signs of having been clouted – it is very vulnerable. Make a similar check on the engine cases. Particularly look underneath. Rocks tend to hit the bottom of an engine, not the

The previous owner has patched up the air filter housing. What went through that crack before he bodged it up?

top where it is far more convenient to view the damage.

17. Examine the air-box and hose from the carburettor to the air-box. If there are any signs of leaks, then be wary of the whole bike. Literally 30 minutes of breathing dusty air will wreck the engine totally. In this respect, we can return to our earlier assessment of the machine's owner. Look at the air-filter element. Is it clean and in good condition? If it isn't, then the bike has been owned by a bodger and ought to be avoided.

By now, you should have a good idea of the state of the bike and the personality of its owner. If the message is that the bike belonged to a caring, meticulous rider then think seriously about purchasing it — even if the price is high. If this message doesn't come through, stay away — even at a bargain price.

## Selling your Bike

Whilst we were discussing this chapter, Bill Brown made an important point and one which many riders forget. Your time is the cheapest commodity and your most valuable asset in the whole bike-selling exercise. For Bill to spend even an hour of his mechanic's time on a bike pushes its price up tremendously because of the wages and overheads involved, yet a private owner can spend a week on a bike for "free".

**Workshop time is very expensive and any repairs the dealer has to make to your part-exchange bike will be paid for by you — directly or indirectly.**

Do make sure that your bike creates the right impression. Buy a new set of cables and oil them. Get some smart new decals for the tank and side panels and give the bike a thorough service so that you can convince the buyer, whether this be a trade or private customer, that yours is the sort of bike he can buy with confidence. Adopting this approach can have quite a radical effect on the value of your bike. Taking two identical machines, one clean, well-kept and clearly cared for, and the other tatty, Bill would value the good example between a third and a quarter higher. In other words, £250–£350 difference on a thousand pound bike and largely through the exercise of some modest effort and thought. Does that sound enough of an incentive to get into the workshop?

# Caring for the beast

BIKE preparation, more than anything else, is the key to happy and successful racing. If you are a hyper-fit, fearless megastar with limitless riding ability but the spokes fall out of the back wheel half way round on your first lap, then all your talents are wasted. Conversely, even a dice for twenty-seventh position in the Junior's race can be a good day's fun if the bike is running sweetly.

Later in the book, we are going to have a look at bike tuning. That is, improving the performance of the motorcycle. However, let us begin by simply getting the machine to function properly. This does not require any great mechanical ability and can prove a lot of fun. I can only pity riders who have someone else to work on their bikes since they miss forming the bond with a bike which only close personal contact can achieve: not unlike consummating the marriage with the first-night nuptials!

Before discussing what we are going to do to the motorcycle, let us think how we are going to achieve our aim. In particular, what tools we need. The great majority of work on any racing bike can be done with a fairly limited range of tools but nevertheless, their initial purchase is expensive.

The first item on the shopping list is a tool box. A standard cantilever design is all that is needed, although my own is rather trick with little wheels at the bottom so it can be rolled around the workshop floor. Even this deluxe version cost only £10.

A tool box is not a bin but a receptacle for holding tools. This is a key point and one which is often forgotten by racers who throw everything into the tool box in the hope that one day it might be required. This is folly and can be irritating in the extreme if one is in a panic trying to repair the bike at a meeting. Instead, plan the placing of the tools logically and don't overload the tool box with junk.

On the top tray, I have my ring spanners. These range from 8 mm–24 mm

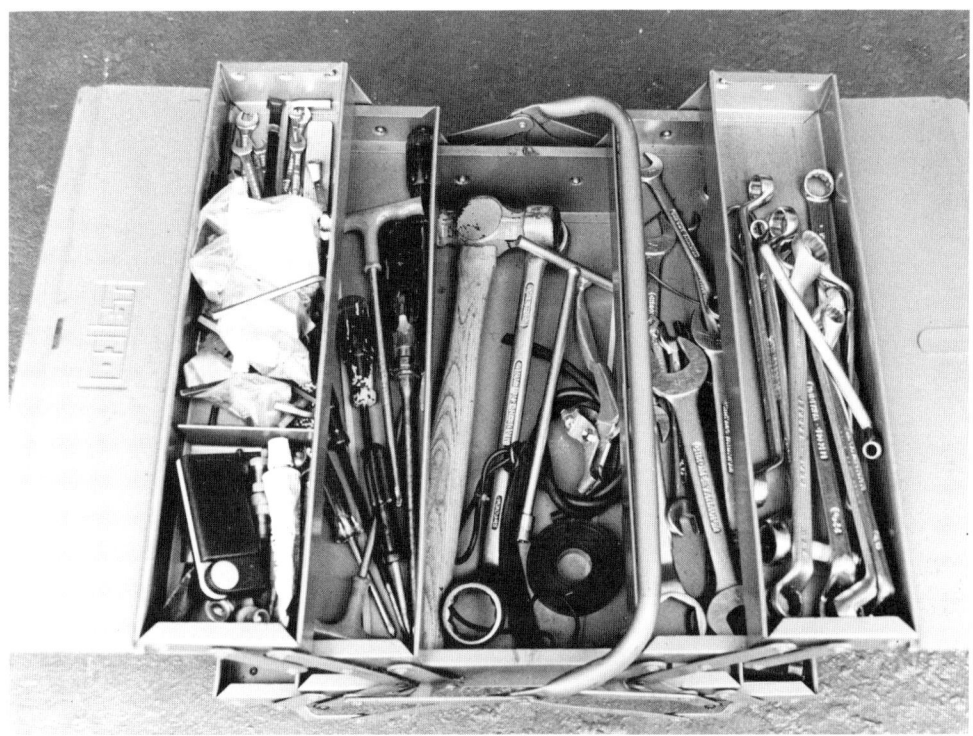

**The author's toolbox. Neat, tidy and accessible.**

which means that I can work on most nuts on most bikes. Ring spanners offer more purchase on a nut than open-ended, so use them wherever possible. Because they are the most used, they are in the most accessible place.

Opposite them in the small compartments are spare plugs, chain connecting links and split links, Allen keys and a selection of nuts and bolts. I also include my tyre gauge in this top tray, in its own box, so that it doesn't get damaged. All these items are fiddly things to find in the bowels of the tool box so I keep them where they are visible.

On the next level are open-ended spanners in the same range of sizes as the ring spanners. Opposite them is a tray of screwdrivers. Chisel pointed in a range of sizes and two T-bars for the Philip's head screws.

**A good quality open-ended spanner – 20 years old and still as good as new.**

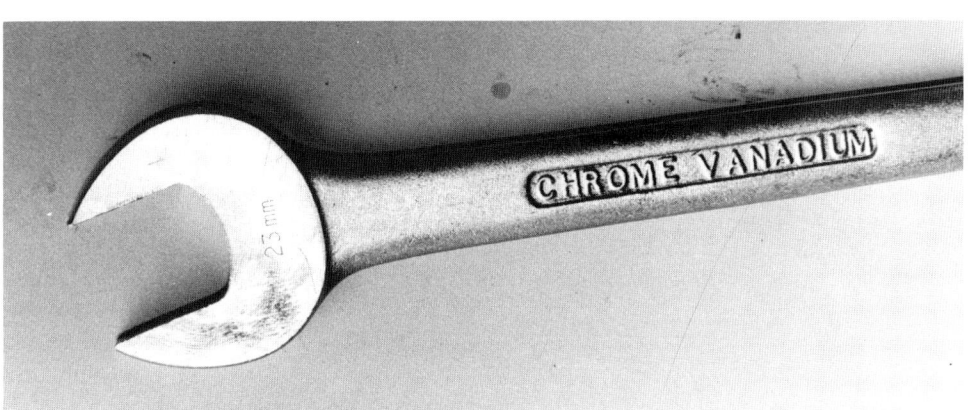

Finally, in the bottom goes a ball peine hammer, spare petrol piping, locking wire and other clumsy bits and pieces. My toolbox has additional compartments on the outside as well and in these are kept "dirty" items such as vice grips, tyre levers and drifts. These can just as well go in the bottom of a small tool box.

This selection of tools should allow all maintenance to be carried out during a meeting and a lot of pre-race preparation too. However, to be sure of being able to tackle the whole bike, two more items are needed.

The first is really a selection of equipment masquerading under one name. This is a socket set. Like the ring spanners, the sockets should all be metric since these nuts are now universal on all modern racing bikes.

**The author's much used but still trusty Elora socket set. 20 years old and still in perfect condition.**

I would always urge any newcomer to purchase the best possible quality tools, since they are the cheapest in the long run. My ring spanners and socket set were bought for my eighteenth birthday and have been used hard for the last twenty years. The ring spanners are made by the British Bedford Company whilst the socket set was manufactured by the equally reputable German firm of Elora. Every item of both sets is as good as new and I firmly believe that they will be in the same condition in another twenty years. The catch is that neither company make cheap — or even modestly priced — tools.

This being the case, try to buy top quality tools at least in the sizes which are most frequently used. For example, a 12/13mm ring spanner and its 10/11mm brother will scarcely ever be out of your hands. Get a Bedford, Elora or some other top-quality spanner in these sizes. Economies can then be made with the socket set and some of the less-popular ring spanner sizes — for example the 14/15mm which, except for the contrary nature of Japanese engineers, need not be in your tool box at all.

**A good quality ring spanner.**

Tools from the Far East are much cheaper than their European or American equivalents and equally, they are of inferior quality. If you are forced to buy cheap tools go for something like the Japanese Draper tools which are not bad — but stay away from the really bargain basement priced Taiwanese and Korean products. These are simply a waste of money.

Finally, every racer needs a torque wrench. This is an extension bar which, when used in conjunction with sockets, can apply a precise amount of force, or torque, to a nut. This is important for two reasons. First, certain items need a required torque for them to work safely. The centre bolt on a clutch has to be tightened down to a safe limit so that it does not work loose, as do certain key bolts on the rear suspension. Another function of torque is to spread the load evenly on a cylinder head so that it does not distort because one of the bolts has been tightened more than another. Finally, certain studs can shear if overtightened. A torque wrench can apply exactly the amount of pressure needed for security without fear of stripping the threads of the bolt or stud.

There are several types of torque wrench available but by far the best is the British Nor-Bar. This clicks at a pre-set torque and works equally well either upside down or at any angle. This feature in itself is very useful when working in confined quarters. Inevitably, Nor-Bar wrenches are expensive but they last forever and are well worth the investment.

Now to the bike itself. Ironically, the easiest way to consider this is by starting at the end. You return from a good day's racing, the bike all covered in clag and the rider completely exhausted. What do you do?

The biggest mistake is to leave the bike in the garage until you are feeling in a more mechanical mood. If you have a power washer and can wash your bike at the meeting, this is ideal, but if you don't, there is no great problem. World championships were won and lost many times before power washers came into vogue and it upsets me to see young riders who should be spending their money on racing and chasing girls worrying about buying luxuries like power washers. They're nice if someone will give you one but don't consider them a necessity.

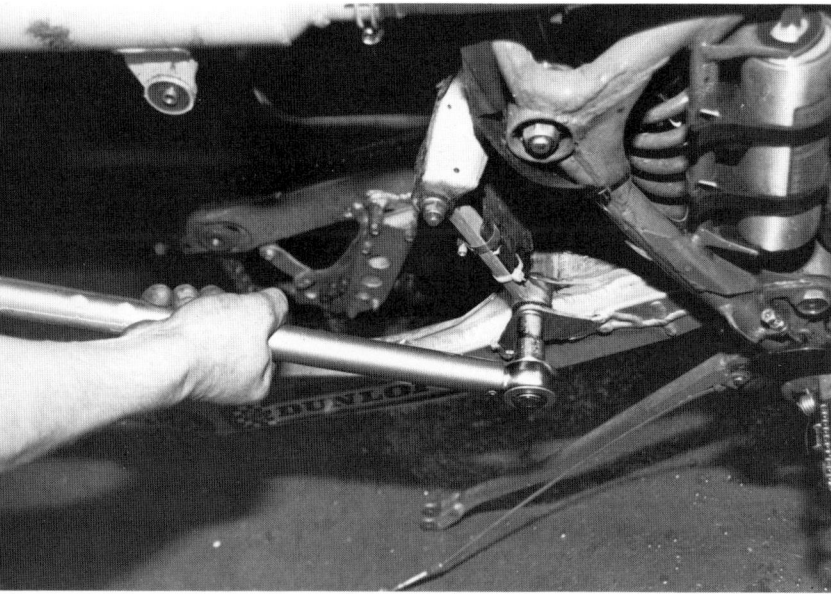

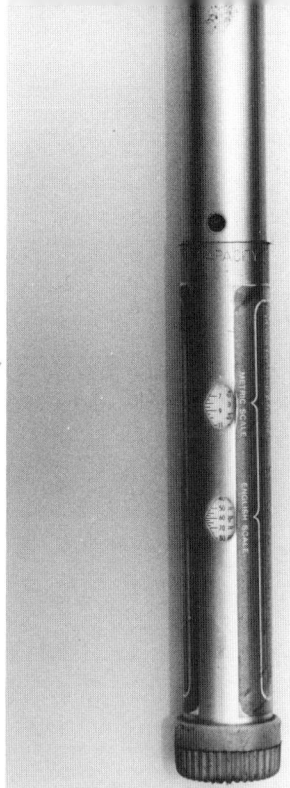

*Above, left:* **Using a torque wrench on a fail-safe bolt, in this case a rear suspension strut.**

*Above, right:* **Close-up of a torque wrench.**

Before starting work, remove the chain since this will rust instantly when washed, being completely free of any lubricant you may have put on during the course of a meeting. If you have not the time to remove the chain completely, then at least give it a good spray with chain lube which will retard rusting and also the ingress of dirt which might be forced into the chain by the water jet.

An ordinary hosepipe and two brushes will do the job just as well. Wrap a bit of polythene round the exhaust and carburettor and use a stiff brush and plenty of water to remove the bulk of the mud. A softer brush can then be applied to the tank, wheels and brake hubs where damage might result from heavy attacks with stiff bristles. For a gleaming finish, give the whole bike a good wash over with some soapy water applied with a soft brush and then hose it off.

Once clear of the meeting's debris, the bike is ready to be worked on. The washing should be done on Sunday night since leaving the job even twenty four hours makes it twice as hard. On Sunday too, the wheels should be removed and wiped dry. Not cleaned, note, but just wiped dry so that the hubs or discs won't rust. A quick spray with a water-repellant is also useful to prevent rusting of plated parts. With the bike in this state, it can be left to be prepared when the rider is more suited to the task since it will neither deteriorate nor make more work.

Now, let us have a look at the maintenance schedule.

Never begin work on a bike without an empty box. An empty five litre plastic oil can with one side cut out is ideal. Into this goes **EVERYTHING** which is removed from the bike. Then at least you can lose them properly later when you are not feeling totally shattered.

Let us begin with the wheels. If the meeting has not been exceptionally muddy,

A bike can be washed and cleaned perfectly with just a hosepipe and a selection of brushes.

Wherever possible, use a ring spanner on nuts since this spreads the load much more evenly around the nut.

**As you work on the bike, put all the bits removed into a clean container. In this case the author has used a redundant vegetable bin.**

give the hubs a clean-out with neat petrol or contact cleaner. Avoid spraying contact cleaner direct on to your hands or breathing it in a confined atmosphere. Equally, do not blow the asbestos dust out of the hubs, since this too, is none too clever for one's lungs. Above all else remember that petrol vapour is highly explosive and a severe fire risk. Keep it away from naked flames and cigarettes.

The same ground rules apply to a disc-braked wheel except that cleaning a disc is quicker and easier. Take care to slip a wedge of soft wood between the brake pads so they do not drop out inadvertantly.

Disc brakes suffer when their hydraulic fluid degrades. Unfortunately, this happens all too easily since hydraulic brake fluid is hygroscopic — it absorbs water — and soon deteriorates. Bubbles in the brake pipe will also cause "sponginess" and to deal with both of these problems, the hydraulic system should be bled regularly, at least once a month — and the brake fluid totally replaced.

If the meeting has been very muddy, strip out the brake cam and clean and regrease it. When removing the brake shoes, do remember to mark them so that they go back in the same position as when they were removed. Brake shoes wear to the shape of the brake drum and their effectiveness is dramatically reduced if they are disturbed. I mark them "top" and "bottom" with a scribe. Take care not to overgrease the brake pivot or cam since grease is the death of a set of brake linings. The linings should always be cleaned down with petrol or contact cleaner before being returned to service.

**Clean the brake drum after every meeting and make sure the front disc is free of grease. <u>Don't</u> spray contact cleaner on to your hands.**

The correct position can easily be found for the brake arm if it is marked with a cold chisel before removal. A gentle tap across the arm and on to the pivot will leave a line which will instantly position the brake arm and save both time and irritation.

Again, if the meeting has been muddy, the rear suspension will need stripping and greasing. Do ensure that all parts are meticulously clean before reassembly since all these systems are under a lot of strain and need to be kept well-lubricated with grease. It is essential to use a racing quality grease for these highly stressed pivots, rather than an ordinary lithium-based automotive grease. All the rear suspension bolts will need to be re-tightened to specific torque settings and these will be in the owner's manual — itself an invaluable aid to painless maintenance.

If the race was run under clean conditions, then the rear suspension can be left alone except for checking the tightness of all nuts. However, if grease nipples are fitted — as is becoming increasingly common — pump some lubricant through after slackening off the retaining nuts on the pivot, of course. Even if grease nipples are fitted, strip and clean the system every four meetings.

Although it seems like more work, the bike is quicker and easier to deal with minus the tank and saddle. Remove these now, taking care not to damage the tank's petrol tap by leaving it on a hard surface or getting dirt forced inside it.

At the same time, drain the gearbox oil. I realise this is easy for me to say since

*Above:* Clean the brake shoes after every race. The front disc pads should also be cleaned. Avoid inhaling the dust from either the shoes or the disc pads.

*Right:* The brake pivot should be lightly greased very regularly.

I get free oil but there is no doubt that a rider can save himself a lot of money by investing in fresh gearbox oil. This can be draining while the rest of the bike is prepared.

Whilst the gearbox is without oil, always stick a piece of duct tape on the tank with the words **'NO OIL'**, written on it. It is very easy to forget that a bike is without oil in the rush to get to a meeting. The results of doing this can be truly horrific. I know!

**'No Oil' reminder when the gearbox is drained.**

Whilst the tank is off, check that the wiring is not being chafed and torque down the cylinder head nuts. In practice, it is extremely unlikely that these nuts will move far but a check does no harm and has a calming effect on the rider. Check the head steady for the same reason.

Check the throttle cable for excessive slack. Personally, I do not subscribe to the theory of having no backlash in the throttle cable. When the carburettor gets

hot or the cable becomes the slightest bit kinked during the course of a race, the engine won't shut off. Instead, aim for about 2mm of play. The throttle should then open smoothly and fall shut of its own weight. This smoothness of operation is critical and can be achieved on any bike providing the throttle drum is clean, the carburettor box and slide undamaged and the cable run smooth. If the action is not perfect, work from the top to the bottom until it is.

About every six meetings, run some oil through the clutch and front brake cables so that these too, are smooth in operation. Do this by making a funnel from Plasticine at the top of the cable and allow gravity to pull the oil through. The dregs from a bottle of two-stroke or gearbox oil are ideal. However, don't put oil in the throttle cable. The "feel" that this transmits is amazingly sensitive to the rider and oil in the cable masks this completely. The clutch and front brake are not nearly so finely tuned and the oil not only adds to their smoothness but also helps keep debris out.

One simple job which should be done every meeting is to drain the carburettor. Dust always manages to get into the float bowl and does no harm if removed regularly. Always support the body of the carburettor with one hand when removing the drain nut so that the rubber manifold is not strained. Whilst in the area, check for any signs of deterioration in the manifold. Tiny cracks will be the first clue which can lead to a split and then instant engine seizure.

The next job is a key one: cleaning the air filter. The "stars" will use four or five air filter elements during a meeting, changing them after every race. This is no doubt the best policy if a rider is scratching for every last bhp but in most meetings, it is just about possible to race on a single filter. Certainly two filters — one for practice and the other for racing — are more than enough.

There are several ways of removing muck and air filter oil from the element. The quickest is to use petrol but this is also the most expensive. Just as good, if slower, household washing-up liquid. Three or four washes and rinses will be needed to remove both the detergent and dirt. The filter should then be wrapped in a piece of absorbent kitchen tissue and left to dry overnight.

When re-oiling the element, use only a recognised brand of filter fluid which is designed for the job. Oil the filter well and then squeeze it hard until it fits inside your clenched fist. A tiny amount of residual oil is all that is needed to act as a filtration medium; any excess will simply clog the filter and reduce performance. The best filter oils are very thin for easy application but do need to be left for twenty minutes whilst they go thick and tacky. If two filters are available, wrap the spare one in a clean plastic bag ready for use at the meeting.

I never fully trust the seal between the element and the air filter box and to make doubly sure of it, I grease this face lightly, which guarantees an airtight junction. With the element fitted, the air box lid can be replaced. Again, I am sceptical about the seal and like to guarantee the integrity of the edges by oversealing them with duct tape. This might seem like an extreme measure except that I have far less dirt get into the air box than riders of similar machines. This means that the filter has less work to do and the motor therefore gives more power for a longer period.

Now is the time to make a general check on the tightness of all the bolts on the bike. Do take care not to overtighten, and until a natural sympathy for how tight a fitting should be is developed, don't be shy of using your torque wrench. A good rule of thumb is that it is always easier to tighten up a bolt a little at a time rather than strip the thread with too much energy too soon. Pay particular attention to

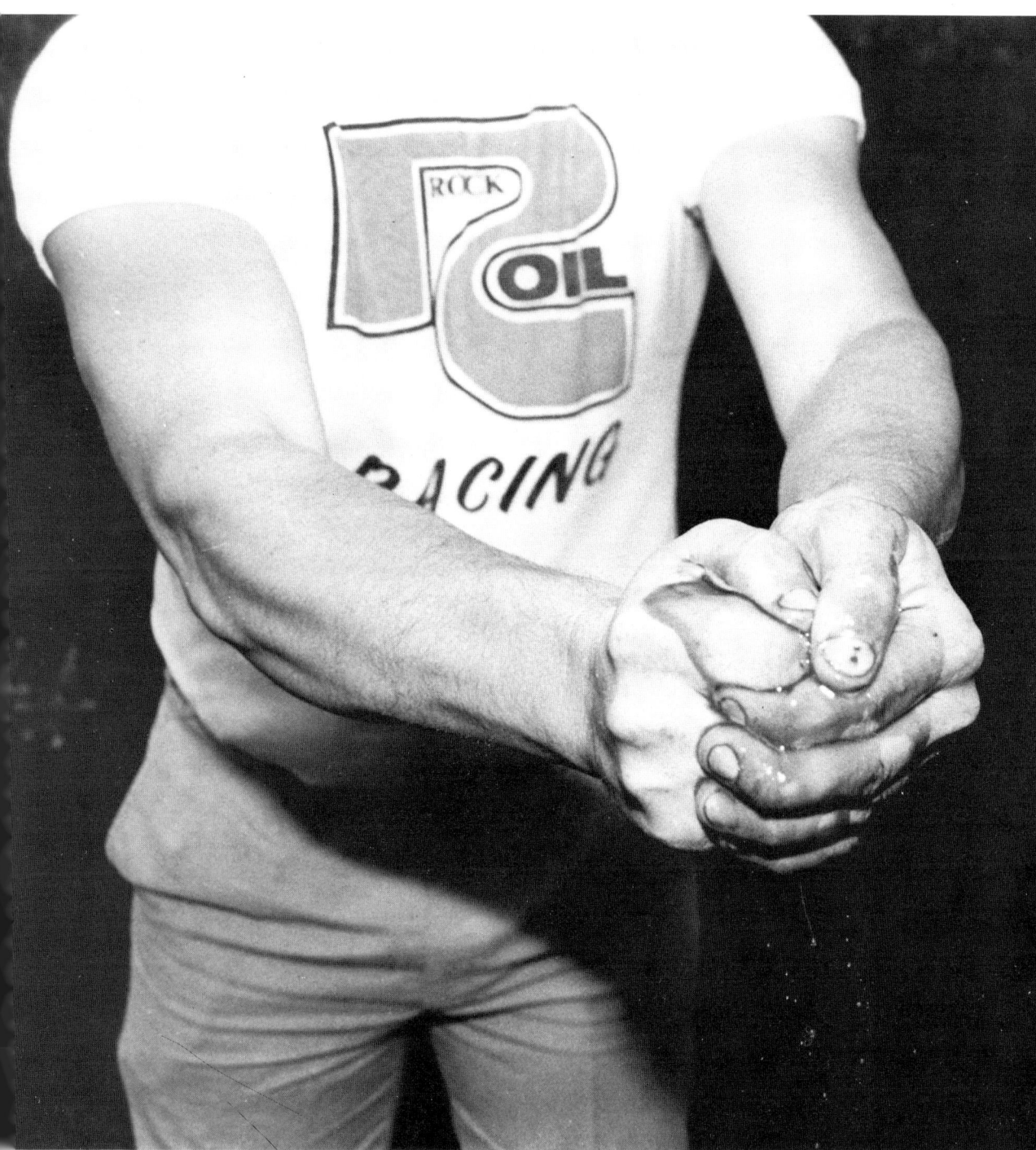

All the oil must be squeezed (but not wrung) out of the air filter element.

the rear sprocket bolts which will invariably have loosened if they have not been assembled using *Loctite*.

Check the steering head bearings for wear in the way described in Chapter Four. Whilst the wheels are out of the bike, keep an eye out for potential wheel bearing wear.

A critical check to make is that the handlebar grips are firm. There is more myth and folklore about this one job than any other in motocross and the solution is simple. When fitting a pair of new grips, clean the 'bars and grips with contact cleaner. Make sure that they are perfectly dry and then apply a liberal coating of rubber tile adhesive to each surface and slide the grips on. They are now permanently attached to the 'bars and nothing whatsoever will remove them. The only problem is that they will have to be cut off when they are worn out and the bars physically scrubbed clean of the adhesive.

Before beginning reassembly, check the level of the radiator fluid and the security of the hoses. The only time to start playing with the radiator cap is when the bike is cold. Since they adjoin each other, a visual check on the front brake master cylinder can also be done at this time along with confirmation that the brake has not suffered any damage.

Although not favoured by top mechanics, I like to grease bolts before reassembly. It is all well and good to fit bolts dry – they are much quicker to clean in this state and torque down more accurately – providing you can guarantee stripping the bike every week. But amateur riders also have to think of their jobs, sleep and meals. A greased bolt will come to no harm if it is left in the bike for months: for example, the pinch bolts on the fork yokes. A dry bolt can corrode and cause expensive damage.

I am also favourably inclined towards *Loctite* for securing all fail-safe bolts. Clean the thread of the bolt and then apply a tiny amount of *Loctite*. The liquid is a form of metal bonding glue which will then retain the bolt indefinitely and also prevent corrosion. All *Loctite* adhesives are **VERY** powerful and should be used sparingly. A tube of *Loctite* lasts me about two years and I use it regularly on saddle retaining bolts, expansion chamber bolts and the head steady: all areas which suffer from vibration.

When replacing the wheels, give each spindle a wipe over with a high melting point grease. This helps fitting and also prevents corrosion occurring between steel and magnesium parts – the front forks are very prone to this unless the wheel is stripped out every week. Do not overgrease the spindle — a light smear is ample — since the excess lubricant will find its way onto the brake shoes with disastrous results.

Once the wheels are in place, the spoke tension can be checked. This is a difficult job for a newcomer to master since it depends entirely on feel. However, be aware that the job needs doing and seek the help of an experienced rider to help you judge whether the spoke tension is correct. As always under, rather than over, tighten.

Finally, two cosmetic but important jobs. First, if anyone is giving you any help, make sure the appropriate stickers are in the right place on the bike and are neat and tidy. Do this even if you have only been given 10p off a bottle of oil.

Second, give the bike a spray over with rust-inhibitor. Not only does the bike look much smarter but mud does not cling to the surfaces nearly so much and parts do not rust on the bike. Used sensibly, a tin should last all season and is a good investment.

Now we are ready to go racing.

# Tuning

BECAUSE this is the complete book of motocross, it is right and proper that it should include a chapter on tuning. However, please do approach this job with caution. Firstly, because it is incredibly easy to make a bike go slower by having it tuned by an amateur — and by not a few professionals either — and secondly, because mistakes can be expensive. Ruin a cylinder barrel and it will take more than a few sober and celibate nights at home before you can afford to race again. In my experience, there are very few mechanics who can improve a motorcycle's performance dramatically and so for help with this chapter, I turned to François Goiffings. In my opinion — and many others involved in motocross professionally — François is the best in the world.

He began life as a rider and was the youngest International in Belgium until a series of accidents forced him out. First working for Raymond Boven, who was riding for the Montesa factory, he then moved on to Honda where he was mechanic for World Champion Graham Noyce — and also the highest paid technician on the Honda team. A true accolade from a Japanese company. François is now *White Power* importer for the Benelux countries and his large tuning factory in Genk is a mecca for riders throughout Europe. He is also a charming and relaxed person — both rare traits in a top tuner — with a courtesy and patience which makes him unique.

Before getting down to facts, François was at pains to point out that in this chapter, we are discussing what he calls "beginner's tuning". There is much more that he does to motors but these tricks stretch into the realms of mechanical magic and are the exclusive domain of G.P. riders and professional mechanics. If you set the bike up as Françcois describes, then it will not be lacking in power or handling!

First the motor. It goes without saying that all motocross motors are good today

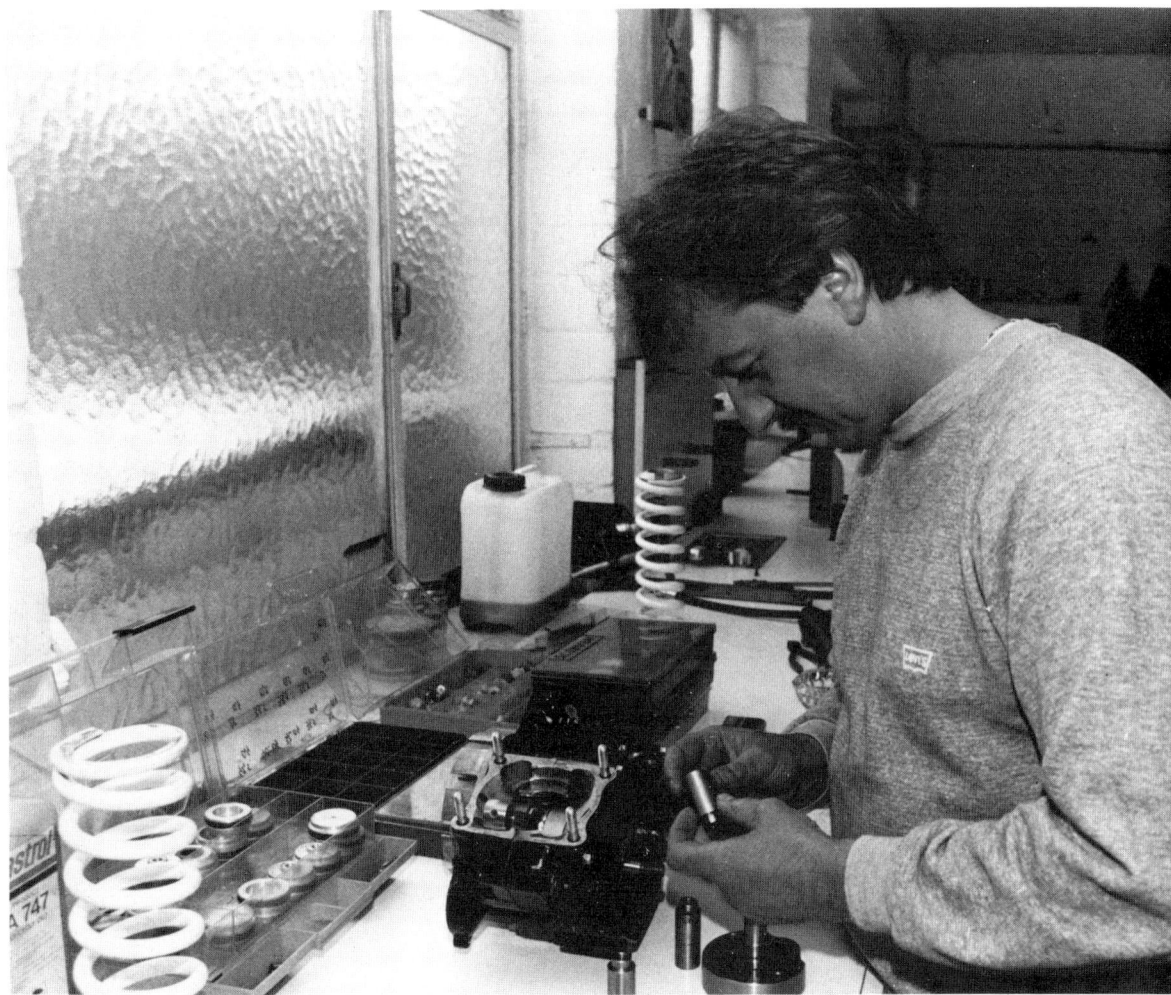

**François Goiffens, 'the world's best motocross tuner', fettles a motor.**

and since most of them are based on grand prix engines their designs are invariably sound. For the private rider to improve them would seem to be an impossibility, but this is not the case for a number of reasons. First and most important is the fact that production engines are built on an assembly line by very ordinary, semi-skilled workers. They bolt all the bits together according to the engineers' instructions and no more. The engines are assembled with all vagaries of any mass-produced item and if your barrel-finisher has had a row with his wife, or drank too much the night before, then your motor is likely to be a slow one.

Second, cost has to be balanced against effectiveness. If item "a" will work nearly as well as item "b", but is 50% cheaper, then the former will find its way into the engine – even if power is sacrificed as a result.

Finally, all engines are built for the mythical "average" rider. This means that they will be fairly powerful, fairly easy to ride and fairly torquey – trying to please

all the people all the time. If you know what you want, then you can extend any of the motor's characteristics in any direction. Even a passing inspection of the barrel will reveal that it is not as the designer intended. The transfer ports will be full of casting irregularities and very often, flash (that is the feathery looking bits of aluminium caused by slight imperfections in the mould), will be visible in the ports. This must be removed. The ports need not be polished, or even glassy smooth, but all the irregularities should be removed. There are several ways of achieving this finish: the faster the job, the easier it is to ruin the barrel!

Professionals employ a high speed drive — usually from a compressor. This will spin at around 24,000 rpm and with a tungsten carbide cutting tool will convert a barrel into a vegetable strainer in the wink of an eye. A high-speed model maker's drill is also a formidable tool. If you do have access to either of these, work very slowly and gently. It is infinitely easier to remove metal than replace it.

Milling tools for use with either a flexible drive or a model maker's drill.

A second best is a flexible drive hooked up to a drill. I used this method driving the tool from my pillar drill at 5,000 rpm before splashing out on a model maker's drill. This permits me to remove the bulk of the metal and then finish the job by hand. Altogether a sensible compromise. A flexible drive and a set of milling tools are not very cheap but are well worth investing in if you propose to do any serious tuning.

Whether a high or low speed cutting tool is used, you *must* wear safety goggles. An aluminium chip leaving a tool at only 5,000 rpm will literally blind you, particularly when the tendency is to peer closely into the barrel to see exactly what is going on.

Finally, there is the finger and file method. Emery paper applied with the finger will remove the metal from the barrel effectively and safely whilst a set of needle files can be used to clean up the casting flash from the ports. This method is slow

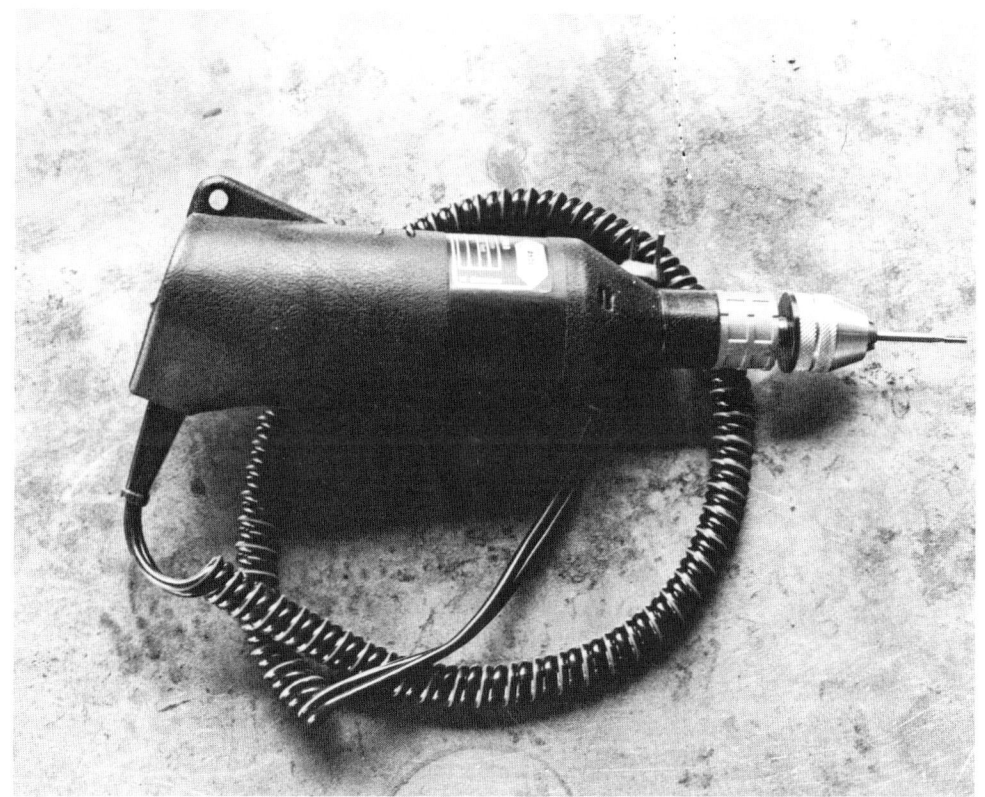

*Above:* A model maker's drill and a good quality milling bit will remove metal almost as fast as a professional's air-driven tool: a potent weapon in the wrong hands!

*Left:* Needle files. Slow but safe.

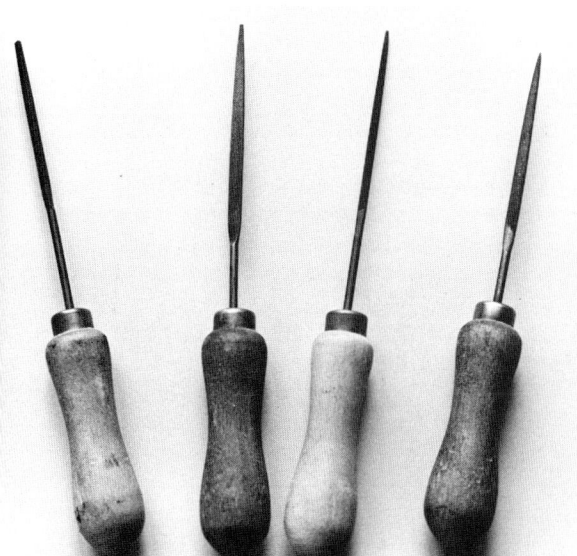

but is by far the best approach for the novice since things happen so much more controllably than when a power tool is employed.

Merely cleaning up the ports will effect a quite dramatic increase in performance – other things being equal – since the bike will now begin to function as its designer intended. Now we can go on to make the motor produce more power.

If the height of the exhaust port is raised, the engine will rev. more freely and produce more power, providing a suitable expansion chamber is employed. Every engine's requirement is different but a typical 500 cc motor will take a rise of about 1 mm without any problem. The barrel must be placed on a face plate and then a centre-punch used carefully to mark three or four guide marks at the 1 mm point. These can then be joined to give a working guide line. When the correct amount of metal has been removed, the edge of the port should be gently radiused, as should that of all other ports in the barrel. This slight radius gives a ramp which allows the piston rings to float in and out of the barrel more easily, thus reducing wear. The big danger lies in making the port too big and François' own solution is to use the shaped port shown in fig. 2.

When the exhaust port is raised, the compression ratio is lowered. This is no bad thing on most motors since many of them – the 500s in particular – suffer from pre-ignition or 'pinging'. However, with the latest oils, several interesting options appear. For example, the cylinder head can be machined to maintain the integrity of the compression ratio and aviation fuel, or Avgas, can be used.

At the time of writing, the highest octane pump fuel available is 99. By contrast, Avgas can be bought with an octane rating of 110. Note however, that not *all* Avgas is rated at 110 – some is 99. All petrol loses some of its octane rating when oil is added but with the latest synthetic and mineral/synthetic composite oils, which are mixed at 50:1 or 60:1, the degradation is minimal. Thus, the mixture burnt is high octane and so much less susceptible to pinging.

However, neither raising the exhaust port, nor raising the compression ratio nor employing Avgas will be of any benefit unless a 'power pipe' is employed. This is an expansion chamber which has been built to resonate most effectively at high rpm – thus making use of the engine's new found willingness to rev. out. Many companies make power pipes and they vary in quality from the truly awful to the quite spectacular. François' own pipes are extremely effective and I have used *Fresco* designs with great success. Clearly, two or three weeks of paddock research is essential before parting with money but if you can find a good rider who is campaigning a quick production bike, then this will serve as a very good guide.

The motor we have built will now be markedly more powerful, or at least it will be potentially a much stronger engine when we have sorted out the carburation. However, before examining this most critical element in motorcycle tuning let us consider the engine's characteristics as they stand.

There will be considerably more power than a normal engine but this will largely be in the mid and upper part of the power range. Cleaning up the transfer ports helps the mid-range and the bottom-end power but raising the exhaust and fitting a power pipe is purely for the top end of the power curve. In fact, the motor might be more difficult to ride.

To make the power more usable, we must look at the reed petals. Earlier, we noted that production engineers often fitted parts which were adequate for the task in hand but not perfect. Nowhere is this more true than in reed petals. My

M9669

(1) EXHAUST PORT 'FLASH'

'LAND' SUPPORTS
PISTON RINGS

M9667

(2) ONLY FOR THE EXPERTS

**François examines one of his own power pipes. A tuned exhaust is essential in any serious search for power.**

own favourites are *Rooster* a small company which revolves around its founder, Bernard Hargreaves. Bernard claims his fibre petals to be the best in the world and I would not doubt him for a minute. What all these reeds do is react with supreme accuracy to the needs of the engine, thus making the motor very flexible at the bottom-end of the power band. This kills the surge of power which makes a tuned engine so hard to ride and so smooths out the delivery. The beauty of consulting a reed specialist is that he can provide reeds to suit almost any track. For fast, dry going, Bernard produces +2 and +4 reeds which resonate least at higher rpm and thus give even more power. G.P. riders are becoming increasingly interested in reed petal technology and companies like *Rooster* now supply the stars with a range of reeds to suit different tracks and conditions.

Finally, on a tuned engine the ignition can be retarded progressively. A reduction of 2° initially, followed by a further one or two degrees after testing, is about right for a start. However, as always, experimentation is essential.

So to the carburettor. In François' words "The single most important item on tuning the bike. You can't spend too much time on getting this right". Unfortunately, tuning the carburation is a very skilled job and demands that the rider be both perceptive and sensitive.

Carburation refers to the correctness of the fuel/air mixture provided by the carburettor. In simple terms, if there is too much fuel, the motor will not produce its potential power, whilst too little fuel will cause over-heating and then seizure. All bikes come from the factory with the mixture set too rich, simply because manufacturers live in fear and terror of some sixteen year old screwing the neck off his brand new 125, melting the piston, and dad getting all upset and launching a law-suit. Thus, the bikes are set up so that they will not seize, but neither will they produce any worthwhile power. The problem is exacerbated by the fact that most motocross engines are two-strokes and by nature, these motors demand perfect carburation.

The easiest way to tune the carburettor for the beginner is to run the bike on a flat field. Mark the throttle with two dots: one for half open and one for one third. A dab of paint on the twist grip and another on the throttle drum at the requisite points is all that is needed. Get the bike warmed up thoroughly and then have a five minutes brisk riding to get the motor clean of any excess oil which might have built up in the crankcase.

The bike should now be run flat out for ten seconds. This is, to let the motor be fed by the carburettor's main jet. At the end of the ten seconds, pull in the clutch and stop the motor with the kill button. Remove the spark plug and examine it: the colour should be a dry light brown.

*Left to right:* **Flat slide from a Mikuni racing carburetter. Also shown is the needle and clip and the needle retainer and its mounting screws.**

When checking the plug, only the centre ceramic should be considered since this is the part of the plug which reveals how the engine is running. The plug's body will always be black. If it is oily black, the engine is being excessively oiled and consideration should be given to reducing the amount of lubricant in the petrol. If the centre ceramic is black and sooty, then the mixture is too rich and the main jet can be reduced progressively. After each reduction, check the carburation again.

A mixture which is too lean — which means that there is insufficient fuel being mixed with the air — will cause the engine to ping. This is shown by a knocking noise from the top of the engine, particularly under load. In this case the plug colour will be white or grey and white. This is a danger signal since a motor run so lean will almost certainly seize.

The main jet controls the engine's performance only in the last third to full throttle rev. band. Below two thirds throttle, the needle jet is the prime element.

Use the guide marks to run the engine at half throttle. As with the main jet, try a ten second run and then check the plug. Also, try accelerating away from corners. The power should be crisp and instant. If there is any hesitation — "fluffiness" is the paddock term — then the mixture can be weakened.

Unbolt the top of the carburettor and the needle can be seen dangling beneath the slide. Remove it, making a note which notch its clip is in. This is critical and the cause of many disputes between clubman riders and their mechanics since it is all too easy to forget who was supposed to be remembering what — and all the notches look the same once the needle is removed. Take care of the spring clip which retains the needle. This always flies off at the speed of light and either gets buried at the bottom of a mountain of cow-clap or descends a rabbit hole never to be seen again. I speak from experience in both cases! Lowering the needle weakens the mixture and raising it has the opposite effect. As always, go one notch at a time and check thoroughly.

Finally, the pilot jet. François made an interesting observation regarding this part of the carburettor and one which I never realised, although being an avid carburation tweaker. The bike is fed exclusively by the pilot jet for about one third of the race. Now, since the jet feeds only approximately the first fifth of the engine range, this might seem surprising, except that it must be remembered that when the throttle is closed, the pilot jet is the only thing which supplies fuel to the motor. Even a G.P. rider must close the throttle for corners and so the one third total is soon built up.

Paradoxically, a motor is most susceptible to seizure when the throttle is closed. All two-strokes depend on oil in the fuel for lubrication and when the throttle is closed, very little fuel reaches the engine. Take the scenario where there is a hairpin corner at the end of a long straight.

The rider hurtles down the straight with the engine at peak rpm, on the main jet. He snaps the throttle closed and slams on the brakes for the bend but the engine is still spinning at 7,000 plus rpm except that now, the only fuel which it is being fed comes from the pilot jet — both the needle and main jets being closed off. If insufficient fuel gets to the motor, it will be starved of lubrication and will seize. Now we face a problem. The pilot jet should always be set as lean as possible for really sharp acceleration out of corners and so a dilemma occurs. Too weak and the motor will seize and too rich and the bike will be dull when pulling away from bends. So what do we do?

François suggests that unless the rider is very perceptive, the pilot jet should be left as standard. Weakness on this jet is sensed by pinging under hard braking after a full throttle run. However, this pinging is hard to detect – especially when maximum concentration is demanded by the act of braking in itself. Weakening the pilot jet is possible but even more than any other modification, take it slowly and easily.

Before leaving the carburettor, the current fad for bigger units should be mentioned. François does not approve of these since the bigger the carburettor, then the slower the gas speed through the body. Those who are not *au fait* with Boyle's Law can now feel regret at having spent physics lessons drawing knobbly tyres instead of paying attention to the teacher.

A bigger carburettor gives more top-end performance but worse mid and bottom-end power. Since motocross bikes – other than 125s – tend not to be used at peak revs., then the disadvantages of a bigger bore carb. tend to outweigh the benefits. Having said that, there is no doubt that a big bore instrument does make dramatically more power.

However, do take note of paddock gossip regarding the air-filter box. If your bike has a reputation for running short of breath, the answer almost certainly lies

**A good power pipe. This one is by Fresco.**

in the air box and filter. Always fit a top-class filter — I personally like *Twin-Air* or *Poly filters* — and make sure that there is sufficient intake area for the filter to be well fed with air.

As a final word on the intake system, do make sure that a top-class air-filter oil is used since this can either make or break the filter. The oil should be thin to apply and then dry out quickly to become both tacky and waterproof. The latter attribute is very desirable since if water does penetrate the filter, a sticking throttle will result and this could have dramatic consequences for the rider.

Now to the chassis. Like the motor, this will be subject to the same problems of production engineering which took the edge of the motor and equally, it can be improved.

First the brakes. The quality of disc pads varies tremendously and it is essential to have 1mm clearance between them and the brake disc. If this clearance is not apparent, then heat will continuously be transmitted to the brake fluid and it will soon boil.

The brake line itself can always be improved by fitting a top-quality replacement. *Goodridge* seem to have cornered the market at present. The best brake line will not expand under braking and will thus make the brake feel more sensitive and immediate in its action.

The plastic outer guard of the brake line is invariably too soft and can be improved by replacing it with a stiffer plastic which will slide through the brake pipe guides more easily.

With the force that a motocross bike can throw up rocks, the master cylinders needs protecting with a guard — if the manufacturer has not done this as standard.

François bleeds and replaces the brake fluid after every meeting since it is hygroscopic — that is, it absorbs water. The more water the brake fluid absorbs, the lower its boiling point will be. Similarly, any air at all in the system will destroy the braking effectiveness. Riders at less than G.P. level could no doubt last several meetings on the same fluid.

Rear brake maintenance is as we described in the chapter on basic bike care. François is very meticulous about free play on the pedal when the rider has his foot over the brake, in the racing stance. A lack of free play will cause the brake to fade very quickly.

Other personal preferences of Honda's top mechanic are an obsession with the spoke tension — "check them every time the bike is ridden" — and a fondness for waterproofing all the electrical connections with silicone sealer. Engine bolts too, are checked after every ride. By now, it becomes clear why G.P. riders finish races and we lesser mortals don't!

As *White Power* distributor for the Benelux countries, it is not unnatural that François should be very concerned with the quality of suspension — particularly since this is probably more important than any other aspect of the bike's performance. Inevitably, the failure of standad suspension items — the rear damper in particular — comes down to the two elements we have mentioned so often in this chapter: compromise and cost. If your bike has an averagely good damper with fairly good settings for your weight and riding style, then you will be lucky. If not, dramatic improvements can be brought about with some thought.

First the rear damper. François points out that the pre-load adjustment on any damper is for fine tuning only. Never apply more than 22mm of adjustment either side of the standard spring setting. If a softer or harder setting is needed, then this must be achieved by changing the spring itself. With the bike stood upright,

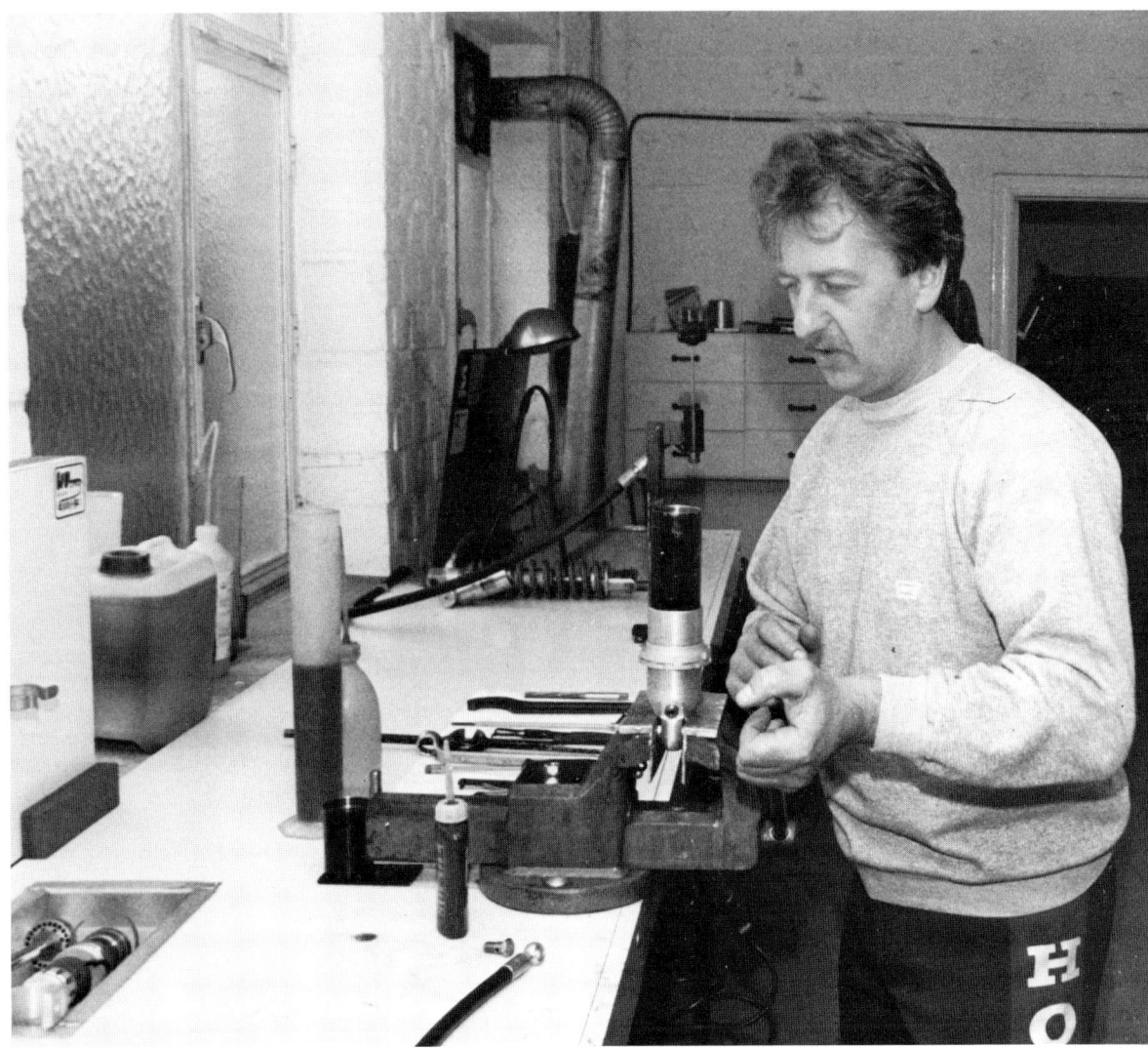

**Françios rebuilds a White Power rear shock. It is essential to seek expert advice for tuning modern suspension.**

and the wheels taking all the weight, the rear damper should settle about 9cm. It should be noted that this is after the spring has been "run-in" — that is, the initial stiffness taken out of it by riding. A good spring will not need more than ten minutes running in.

Setting up a damper is difficult since few riders know exactly what is happening to the bike, and what to ask for to improve the handling. Still fewer mechanics know how to achieve these requirements. Consequently, expert advice **MUST** be sought. The following comments are to help you seek that advice in a lucid and articulate manner.

Big bumps, widely spaced, need plenty of rebound damping so that the shock

has time to return to its fully extended position without excessive speed. Small, sharp, bumps require much less rebound damping so that the shock can react quickly and accurately to the demands placed on it. Clearly, if the spring is too hard, then an excessive amount of rebound damping will be required to prevent the shock being permanently on full extension. This in turn will limit the range of available movement so that it will be impossible to make full use of the potential wheel travel.

At the other extreme, a spring too soft will require an excessive amount of compression damping. This is not desirable since too much compression damping, applied through indent setting on the damper, causes excessive heat and will lead to shock fade.

Again, any radical departure from the standard setting by adjusting either the compression or rebound damping is undesirable since it is, in effect, making the shock perform outside its limits. It is better by far to have the damping modified and use the external adjustment for fine tuning only. It should be noted that all of the Grand Prix quality dampers can be altered to an almost infinite degree and further, their expensive purchase price is somewhat ameliorated by the fact that they can be rebuilt. This is not always the case with mass-produced units.

Front forks are much simpler to work with and can be tuned quite effectively with nothing more than a selection of oils, plenty of thought and some patience. First, what do you want the forks to do?

Before some wit answers "Stop me getting tired at the end of 20 minutes moto", let me say that the question is rhetorical. The forks must absorb a whole range of activities from the plummet off a vertical drop to fine stutter bumps. As always, no fork will do everything perfectly and a compromise is the answer. The most dangerous thing is for a fork to bottom out harshly. When this occurs, the rider is surely heading for a trip over the handlebars. So, to prevent this happening, there must be sufficient oil in the forks and it should be of a suitable thickness. The bike's manual will give a starting guide to both these parameters and clearly this is the place to begin.

The fork action can be stiffened by increasing the oil level, or quantity, in each fork leg. The more oil, the greater the period of time the valving will be exposed to the damping medium, and thus the firmer the action will be. This is the best way to achieve the correct action since it can be finely adjusted merely by adding, or removing, very small quantities of oil. The other way is to alter the weight of the oil in the forks. The thicker, or more viscous, the oil then the harder it will be for the damper valve to move through it and so the stiffer the action. However, even with the best modern suspension fluids, a change from 5W to 7½W is quite dramatic. When such a change is made, the oil levels will have to be re-set again.

At the start and end of the season – or in winter if you are a masochist who likes freezing to death – changes of oil weight will have to be made but from April to September, concentrate on oil levels. The object is to use the maximum amount of travel the forks offer for the most time possible – commensurate with avoiding bottoming the forks over big jumps. There is a temptation to try to do this by using the air caps. Don't! Air is a most ineffective springing medium in that it stiffens the spring rate dramatically as it is compressed. In fact, it is best removed altogether from the forks and there is only one way to do this: with the front wheel clear of the ground. An amazing number of riders bleed the air clear of the forks by compressing them which is the worst thing they could do, since this creates a vacuum which sucks the oil up the fork tube. If a stiffer spring rate is required, use a new spring.

I will conclude by reiterating that some of the things we have discussed in this chapter are difficult to achieve. The comments I have made are not so much instructions for the beginner as notes about things which might be tried as more experience is gained. Certainly, there is an awful lot which can be done to a standard bike which can transform its performance — and make riding more enjoyable too.

# Tyres and tyre fitting

IN the good old days — or perhaps they weren't really so good after all — riders had only two choices to make regarding tyres. Either you fitted a 4.00 x 18 Dunlop Sports rear tyre and a 3.00 x 21 front, or you didn't race. There were no other options. Now, a top Grand Prix rider might test as many as twelve different tread patterns and/or compounds before deciding which is the optimum for a given track.

One thing has not changed from the 1950s. The world's leading tyre manufacturer is still Dunlop. What is different today is that they have rather more than one tyre pattern and two sizes to offer. The range of options is now bewildering, and for guidance through the maze, I turned to Stuart Wyss, who is Dunlop Tyres' Motorcycle Sales and Marketing Manager and one of Britain's leading authorities on motocross tyres.

Tyres are critically important to success — one could argue even rider safety — so choosing them needs a lot of thought. It might be that a compromise will have to be made and there is nothing wrong with this at all. Not every rider has a factory budget and it is better to race on a tyre which is less than ideal, than not race at all. The key is to be well informed so that the most intelligent choice of tyre your budget allows can always be made. As you become more proficient, you will become more discerning as well. It is at this stage that the advantages of having the best tyre, as distinct from an adequate tyre, becomes most apparent.

With the present sophistication of tyres, it is important to remember that there is no 'perfect' tyre. In fact, you will often hear Grand Prix riders saying that their 'hardcross' or 'sand tyre' worked well for twenty minutes and then the track changed making the tyre unsuitable.

Bike manufacturers have the same problem. Regardless of what tyre they fit, it is certain to be less than ideal for most expert riders. So, rather than trying to choose a tyre which will meet with the approval of the aces, they opt for an "average" tyre which will give acceptable performance under a range of conditions and although less than the ultimate, will nevertheless be safe for all riders to use on all tracks. This tyre is called the intermediate and is the one which most bikes come fitted with as standard.

**A Dunlop K990 sand/soft terrain tyre.**

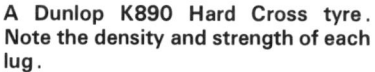

A Dunlop K890 Hard Cross tyre.
Note the density and strength of each
lug.

However, there are exceptions. For example, all the top ten riders in the 1984 500 cc World Motocross Championship used Dunlop tyres and in particular, the *K690A*, a soft terrain tyre that was the centre of incredible interest. The result was a lot of market pressure to have the tyre that the Grand Prix riders worshipped and as a result, the *K690A* found its way on to production bikes. This was very pleasant indeed for purchasers who were running their bikes on soft going but hard luck for those whose local track was like concrete. So remember, even with original equipment, things may not be as straightforward as they seem.

Perhaps the easiest way of explaining the different tyre types is to consider both extremes. The compromise tyre in the middle will then be the mix of the two types: that is, the intermediate tyre which often comes with a new bike.

It is important to remember that a tyre's characteristics are a mix of a number of properties. Amongst these are the compound, or the hardness or softness of the rubber used, and the shape of the knobbles on the tyre and their spacing. These latter are known as the tyre pattern. Then there is the construction of the tyre carcass — the actual body of the tyre on to which the lugs are vulcanised.

Let's start with an examination of the *K690A*, since this became a famous tyre in its day. The first thing to notice is that the knobbles, or lugs as they are more properly known, are small. This is so that the pressure on them is high and they are forced into the soft ground on which the tyre works best. They are arranged in a paddle pattern which gives bands of rubber across the tyre which can grip the sand, or soft earth, and propel the bike forward.

In between the lugs are large empty spaces called seas. It might seem that these areas do nothing but they fulfil two vital purposes. First, when the lugs have been forced into the ground, the large areas of tyre sea stop the tyre cutting deeper and deeper. In fact, they encourage it to float on top of the ground so that there is the minimum drag. Thus, with the lugs cutting into the earth and the sea keeping the bulk of the tyre from sinking, the best possible compromise between traction and flotation is achieved.

The seas also allow the lugs to flex. Note how the lugs are shaped rather than just formed in regular squares or rectangles. This shaping both enhances their ability to grip the earth and also prevents them becoming clogged with mud.

The tread is then vulcanised on to the tyre carcass. This is a circle of rayon or nylon cords arranged in a cross-ply pattern. Where the tyre meets the rim, there

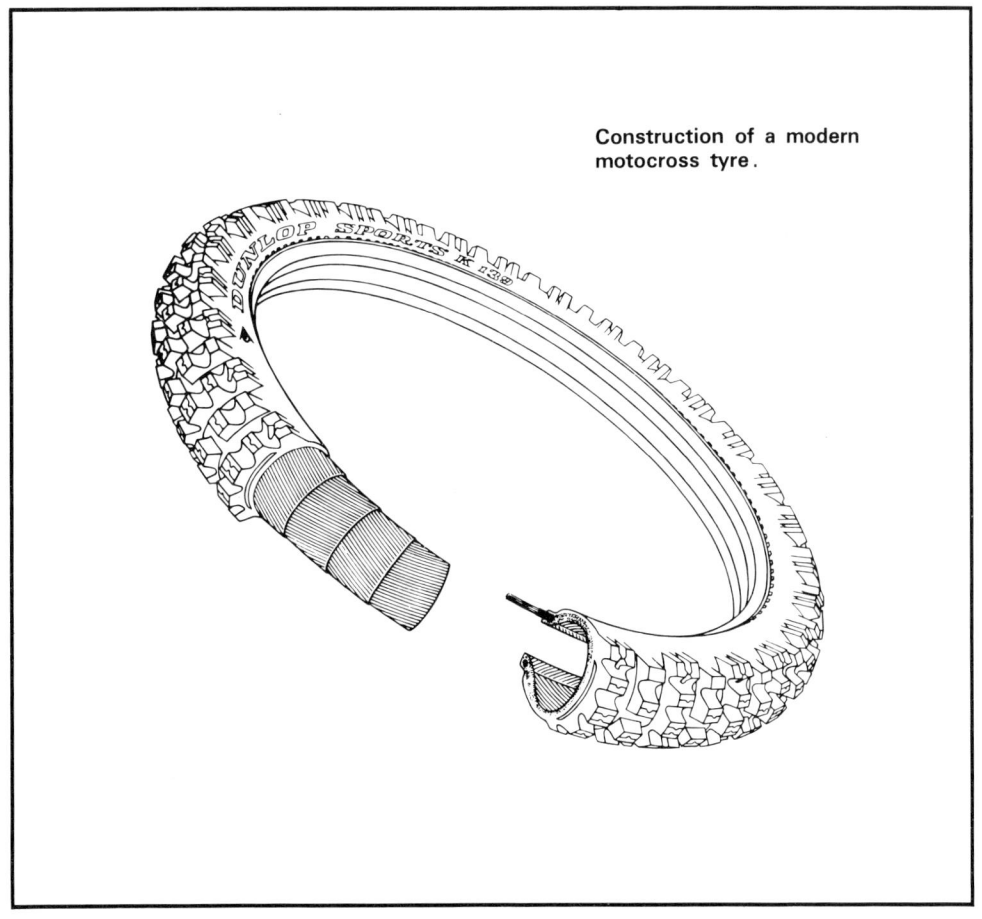

**Construction of a modern motocross tyre.**

are the loops of high tensile steel called the beads. All motocross tyres are extremely rugged and very resistant to being punctured by rocks or even the shock of landing. This extreme strength makes them hard work to fit — which we will discuss at length later — and also explains their cost.

Now to hard tyres. In some ways, the design of a hard tyre is much more challenging than that of a soft tyre. The biggest problem is to make the tyre grip since it is much more difficult to force the lugs into hard ground than it is into soft.

Dunlop designers combat this problem by providing a much greater area of land and therefore rubber contact with the surface of the terrain. In this way, even if the lugs do not penetrate the ground, there will be enough rubber in contact with the surface to provide traction, rather like a road tyre that has a lot of rubber touching the tarmac.

This time the slots in the tyre are there to promote "feel" as well as to allow the lugs to clean themselves. This is one element which Dunlop designers have most trouble appreciating, despite all their computer aided design techniques. All racing tyres have to feel right to the rider and often a racer cannot explain precisely why he likes a tyre. A skilled designer watches the bike in action, listens to the rider and then uses his high technology equipment to produce the answer. Not an easy task.

A further reason for keeping the land area high on the hardcross tyre is lug "wind-up". This is a characteristic known to many riders and is manifested by the lugs of the tyre stretching excessively. This can happen when a soft terrain tyre is used on hard going and is asked to perform on a surface which gives too much drive for the small lugs. When this happens traction is reduced when the bike is vertical and horrific tyre wear results. When lugs wind up with the bike heeled over, the results can be disastrous.

In the middle of the two extremes is Dunlop's *K490* which will provide good, safe performance under a wide range of conditions and is often fitted as standard equipment by manufacturers. Here, the lugs are spaced sufficiently widely to allow a good self-cleaning action and penetration of soft surfaces but they are large enough in size to give plenty of rubber contact with a hard surface. The lugs themselves are hard and give good stability when power is applied with the bike leaned over and the carcass is as stiff and puncture-resistant as either of the specialist tyres.

Now to the choice of tyres. Clearly, if you want to win, then you must have a specialist tyre. Opinions differ as to what riders consider is the best tyre at any given moment but common-sense indicates that you must look at who is winning at the top level to make a sensible choice.

As well as the make of tyre, the sizes are important. Unless the rider is extremely experienced, it is better to follow the manufacturer's recommendations since they usually know what is best for their bike. For example, it might be thought that a bigger tyre will always provide more grip. Unfortunately, this is not always necessarily what a rider needs. It is easy to fit a huge rear tyre on a 125 and go slower simply because the little engine will not spin the back wheel when required and will effectively be bogged down by it.

At the same time, the small rim will distort the large tyre's carcass and prevent it having the correct side-wall stiffness. Better by far to keep to the manufacturer's recommendations.

A further complication regarding tyres is the new form of sizing which is now in operation. The sizes 4.50 x 18 and 5.00 x 18 refer to the tyre's size — the 4.50 its

A Dunlop K490 Intermediate tyre — a good compromise between the hard and soft terrain tyres. This is the tyre fitted as standard on many motocross bikes.

width — and its diameter — the 18. Or at least they did at one time!

The system worked best when tyres were round but now they are anything but. The carcass is most certainly circular but the tread is formed in what is often egg shape. That is, it is wider than it is tall. This is called the tyre's aspect ratio. The numbering system is very complex and rather than try to describe in depth, Stuart Wyss has produced a useful conversion chart (fig. 2) which covers all the most common sizes found in motocross.

Finally, to tyre pressures. There is no firm rule regarding pressures and rider preference plays an important part in the final choice but there are some guide lines which will at least get you started in the right area.

The *more* pressure in a tyre, the less grip it will give. So why not run tyres at 2 psi or 3 psi? Unfortunately the *less* pressure there is in a tyre, the greater the liklihood of a puncture and the more the tyre distorts. So, as in many of the other aspects of tyre choice we have discussed, pressures are a compromise.

The reason for the increased chance of a puncture is that with less air in the tyre, its wall becomes effectively more flexible. When a rider lands after a jump, the force exerted on the tyre is tremendous and if there is not sufficient stiffness

# DUNLOP MOTOCROSS TYRE FITMENT *EQUIVALENTS

| ENGINE CAPACITY | | Code Designated Size (OLD INCH SIZES) | Inch Low Section | 80 series Millimetric | 90 series Millimetric | 100 series Millimetric |
|---|---|---|---|---|---|---|
| Up to 80cc (1) | Rear | | 4·10-14 | 110/80-14 | 110/90-14 | 90/100-14 |
| | Front | 2·75-17 | | 80/80-17 | 80/90-17 | 70/100-17 |
| (2) | Rear | | 4·10-16 | | | 90/100-16 |
| | Front | 2·75-19 | | | | 70/100-19 |
| (3) | Rear | 300 or 350-18 | 4·10-18 | | | |
| | Front | 275 or 300-21 | | 90/80-21 | 90/90-21 | 80/100-21 |
| 125cc | Rear | 3·50-18 | 4·10-18 | 110/80-18 | | 100/100-18 |
| | Front | 3·00-21 | | 100/80-21 | 90/90-21 | 80/100-21 |
| 250cc | Rear | 400 or 450-18 | | 120 or 130/80-18 | 120/90-18 | 110 or 120/100-18 |
| | Front | 3·00-21 | | 100/80-21 | 90/90-21 | 80/100-21 |
| 500cc | Rear | 450 or 500-18 | 5·10-18 | 130 or 140/80-18 | | 110 or 120/100-18 |
| | Front | 3·00-21 | | 100/80-21 | 90/90-21 | 80/100-21 |

*NB: These are typical fitments from International Dunlop Tyre ranges for the cc groups shown.

Not all the above sizes will be available in every territory where Dunlop tyres are sold.

in the tyre wall, it will collapse and allow the inner tube to be pinched between the ground and the wheel-rim. This is called a concussion, or compression, burst, and is the most common way of puncturing a tyre in a race since despite the very hard conditions found on a motocross track, the tyres are tough enough not to be cut.

The lack of stiffness caused by low air-pressure will also mean that the tyre's shape can be distorted. Thus, when the rider gets a lot of power coming out of a fast corner, the tyre can actually be pulled off the rim slightly causing a loss of stability.

Low pressures will also cause the tyre to creep and to prevent this, the wheel-rim is roughened or security bolts are fitted. These are clamps which hold the tyre to the rim and prevent the inner-tube being dragged along – a situation which will eventually cause its valve to be ripped out.

Taking an intermediate tyre, such as the Dunlop *K490* we were discussing earlier, a good starting point would be 12 psi for the rear and 10 psi for the front – these being the pressure suitable for a damp track, without any really big jumps and with a rider in the 140–160 lb range. If the track had some really nasty jumps in it, then the pressures would need to be higher. Similarly, if the going was concrete hard, concussion bursts would be a problem and the pressures should be raised.

Conversely, a tight, slow muddy track with adverse cambers and no jumps worth noting would place a premium on grip and then tyre pressures could be lowered. In such conditions, 6 psi in the front tyre and 8 psi in the rear might be possible.

## Tyre Fitting

It is with some embarrassment that I write this next section. The one task I loathe is tyre fitting. I can fit tyres but will do so under only extreme duress, preferring to swop some skill which I find both pleasant and easy with one of those gifted souls who can flick a tyre on rim with less effort than it takes me to find the tyre levers. Colin Jones, a long standing friend of mine and a top-class enduro rider, showed me yet again the secrets of tyre fitting. He can change a tyre and replace the wheel in the bike in less than five minutes so this art can be mastered. Perhaps I just look at tyres in the wrong way.

1. First let out all the air from the tyre by removing the Schrader valve insert. It is essential that every last breath be removed since racing tyres are stiff enough with any air assistance. Then slacken the security bolts and push them into the inner tube until they are free to remove up and down.

2. A vital point that Colin stressed is that if the work gets hard, you are doing something wrong so stop and work out the problem.

3. First break the bead on the tyre by standing on it until it comes away from the rim. A better way is to run the bike round the paddock with all the air out of the tube since this warms up the tyre nicely and helps it flick off the rim in a flash. Stuart Wyss, of Dunlop, strongly disapproves of this tactic.

4. Carefully insert three small tyre levers under the rim, making sure that they are not in contact with the inner tube. They should be about 4–6 inches apart. Start with the middle one, pulling it right back so that it lifts the bead over the tyre rim. Then, keeping the bead over the rim, progress with the other two. When all three have lifted the bead, the middle one can be removed and inserted further down the tyre. The easiest place to start the exercise is opposite the valve since this is where there is most slack in the tyre. Take very small 'bites' with the levers and keep pressing the tyre into the well of the rim with your feet. The more of the tyre there is in the well of the rim, the easier it will be to remove.

*Above:* **Then insert the tyre levers. They should not be too far apart.**

*Facing page:* **First, break the bead on the tyre by standing on the tyre. An old tyre makes an excellent rest to avoid damage to the wheel hub.**

*Left:* **Ease the tyre off, making sure that the part of the tyre still on the rim is being forced into the well, or centre, of the rim. If you don't do this, it won't come off!**

*Right:* **When the tyre is off on one side, remove the inner tube.**

4. When the tyre is off one side of the rim, pull out the inner tube and then remove the opposite side in the same way. The tyre can be pulled free.

5. Check that the inner tube is in perfect condition and that there are no signs of impact damage or chafing. Give it a thorough dust down with talcum powder and check that the rim tape is not worn. Note: the rim tape should always go over the security bolts not around them as I have sometimes seen.

7. Give the tyre a thorough lubing with tyre lubricant. By far the best product to use is professional tyre soap — this is what the tyre fitters at Dunlop employ. However, failing this, a solution of very soapy water will do. Don't be tempted to use liquid soap since this will corrode the rim and also the valve stem. Don't spare the tyre lube no matter what you use since otherwise, the tyre won't go on.

6. Inflate the tube with just enough air to give it shape. It doesn't need very much. Place it inside the tyre and thread the valve through the rim and lock it in place on the first few threads of the valve stem nut. When the tyre is finally fitted, this nut will be removed since it is advantageous for the valve to be able to move as the tyre creeps since this movement will prevent it from tearing out of the tube.

The tyre can then be eased off the other side and the wheel pulled through.

*Below:* Inflate the inner tube just enough to give it shape.

8. Now the tyre is well lubed, make sure the security bolts are inside the tyre on the side you propose to fit first, but not tightened down. Begin pushing the tyre on by hand until it becomes stiff and then gently ease it with the tyre levers, as always, taking small bites and making sure the already fitted portion is down in the well of the rim. As with the removal, it is just as well to start the fitting opposite the valve.

*Above:* The tyre can be refitted again, taking small 'bites' with the tyre levers and keeping the tyre pressed down into the well.

*Below:* Eventually, the tyre should look like this, with the bead lying parallel to the rim. If it doesn't, become a proficient welder and then you can swap your services with someone who can make the tyre behave.

9. The reverse side can be tackled in just the same way taking great care to ensure that the security bolts are pushed well into the inner tube so that the bead can settle on to the rim. Avoid using the tyre levers on the last few inches of the fitting since this is when the tube is most likely to be pinched. Instead, either tread the tyre home or belt it over the rim with a hide mallet. This job has become infinitely easier since the advent of good tyre lubricants.

10. Finally, inflate the tyre and make sure that the bead is on straight. This may be determined by looking at the fine moulded line on the tyre wall which should be exactly parallel to the rim all the way round. You can try over-inflation to help blow it out but don't go above 50 psi. Instead, deflate the tube and re-lube the rim for a second go. Finish by tightening the security bolts.

Colin can flick a tyre on whilst he gossips and he says that the key to success is three or four days intensive practice after which the skill is never forgotten. This seems good advice but failing this, try to develop some skill which you can trade with someone who has mastered the art.

# Getting to the meeting

THE only bad thing about a motocross bike is that it is such a thoroughbred beast that it only functions happily on the motocross track. Unfortunately, this means that it has to be transported to meetings, since the days when riders used their trusty BSAs for commuting, grass- track racing, road- racing or scrambling as the mood took them, are long since past. The super- specialised modern motocross machine demands to be carried to the track in luxury.

In this chapter, we will look at the two main ways of getting bike and rider to the race. These are a van and a car and trailer. It is also possible to put a bike on a tow- bar mounted rack but most adult motocross machines are too heavy and big to consider this option seriously. First, the van. Without doubt, a van is the best way to get a bike to the meeting. There is ample room in a small van for at least three bikes and all the riding gear, thus opening up the possibilities of cost sharing.

Regarding splitting travelling expenses, let me offer a word of caution. Potentially, going to a meeting with your mate can save you both a lot of money and also make the day's racing more fun: but there are dangers. Before you go, decide who is boss in the van — this should always be the van's driver/owner — who is paying what to whom — and most of all, what will be the seating arrangements. Some of the bitterest rows I have ever witnessed have been as a result of one rider's girl friend having to sit on a 20 litre petrol can, snuggled up to a 490 Maico, whilst the other rides in imperial luxury on the front seat. To the racers, who sits where is almost an irrelevance but often a back seat amongst the oil and riding gear can be the final straw in a delicately balanced female relationship.

There are now a number of mid- sized vans on the market from both European and Japanese manufacturers, all of which will carry a bike to meetings quite

**The Ford Transit 100L van with long wheelbase chassis. There is the option of a 2 litre petrol engine or a 2.4 litre diesel.**

happily. However, of the whole selection, one stands out as being the best choice. That van is the Ford *Transit*: rugged, reliable and now, after a 20 year life span, available at prices from a few hundred pounds upwards.

For help with this section, I turned to Tony Murphy, the Managing Director of C.D. Bramhall of Warrington, one of Britain's biggest Ford dealers and a specialist in *Transit* vans since their introduction. Tony had many useful comments to make not only about the principles of buying a second-hand van but also consumer law relating to what are known as light commercials.

This section is concerned with budget van buying so naturally we are looking at second-hand vans. The same rules apply to making a purchase as they do when buying a second-hand bike. Deal privately and you are on your own: buy from a dealer and potentially you have some protection. I say potentially because if you do buy from a dealer, it is essential to make it clear that the van is being bought as a private vehicle for use as your own private transport. It might seem impressive to claim that you are a pro-racer, going racing for a living, but if you do give this impression to the dealer you leave yourself wide open to losing your protection under the Sales of Goods Act. The reason for this is that a van used for commercial purposes does not carry the same degree of consumer protection as a private car. Whilst a company like Bramhall would not enforce this distinction in the case of an amateur racer, some less scrupulous dealers might well see this as an opportunity to evade their responsibilities.

The guidelines we are going to discuss apply not only to *Transits* but to all vans, but before discussing these in detail, it is worth mentioning that all the *Transits* are worth buying second-hand with the exception of those fitted with the fuel-thirsty V4 engines which were phased out in 1974 when the new body shape was introduced. Other than avoiding this power plant, the rest of the range can be bought in confidence since from their introduction, they have been exceptionally reliable and successful vehicles — which is why one sees so many ancient *Transits*

still tottering about, loaded to bursting point.

The first thing to remember about buying a van is that appearances can be deceptive — very deceptive indeed. Look for an "honest" vehicle — one whose appearance is consistent throughout and matches the van's supposed history.

Let me give an exaggerated example. The vehicle in question is an eight year old *Transit*. The paint-work is immaculate, the engine compartment spotless but there are numerous dents on the inside of the body panels and the seats are oily and torn. The mileage is shown as 60,000. According to the owner, prior to him having the vehicle, it had been used for light delivery work by a dry cleaning company. Apparently an ideal vehicle but let us think a little deeper.

**The inside of a standard Ford Transit van.**

First the age and mileage. The van has been used commercially and has only done 7,500 miles a year. This means one of two things. First, it has been employed on short, intensive journeys, a few miles from base, which will have played havoc with the power unit and gearbox. Second, it may have been "clocked". This is the motor trade expression for a vehicle which has had its odometer either changed or altered to show a lower mileage than the vehicle has actually covered. "Clocking" is illegal and persons convicted of the offence receive jail sentences as a matter of course. Alternatively, the mileage shown may in reality be 160,000 since when odometers reach 100,000, they return to 000,000 again and begin counting afresh.

The second point to consider is the condition of the paintwork. A privately-owned and used *Transit* might retain immaculate body work for eight years but the chances of a commercial vehicle managing this are extremely slim. So has the vehicle been re-sprayed and is the new paintwork hiding rust repaired with fibre-glass and filler? Look underneath the van for signs of over-spray where the sprayer has not masked the area perfectly and paint misses the intended target. A good look underneath the van will also reveal whether filler has been used on the sills or wings.

Next, the impressively oil-free engine bay, a clear sign of an immaculately kept motor? Perhaps so or maybe not. For £5.00, an engine-bay can be steam cleaned to "as new" condition. Have a good look at the rocker box cover for signs of oil leaks and once again, get under the van for a better idea of whether that apparently immaculate appearance can be substantiated.

Then there are the dents in the van side panels. If the vendor's story is true, dry cleaned clothes could not have caused the damage, so how did it occur? And what about the oil on the seats? Someone delivering dry-cleaning would be clean themselves and the seats should be immaculate.

This tale is fictional and exaggerated but it becomes clear that all aspects of the van's appearance and history must be considered because sadly, the world of second-hand vans is full of sharks just waiting to snap up the innocents. Do think before you buy and do take a friend with you to help balance your enthusiasm for getting a vehicle. Perhaps more so than when buying a bike, consider the benefits of buying from a reputable dealer who, by the force of law and his need to protect the company's reputation will be selling the straightforward van it purports to be.

One final factor to be considered when purchasing a van is the status of its previous owner and the use to which the van was put. The hypothetical example I gave earlier of a van used for delivering dry cleaning and therefore not being subject to internal damage serves to illustrate that the van's previous use can radically affect its condition. The ideal van to purchase is one which has been

**Loading a bike easily and comfortably into a van. One person each side of the bike lifts on the fork legs.**

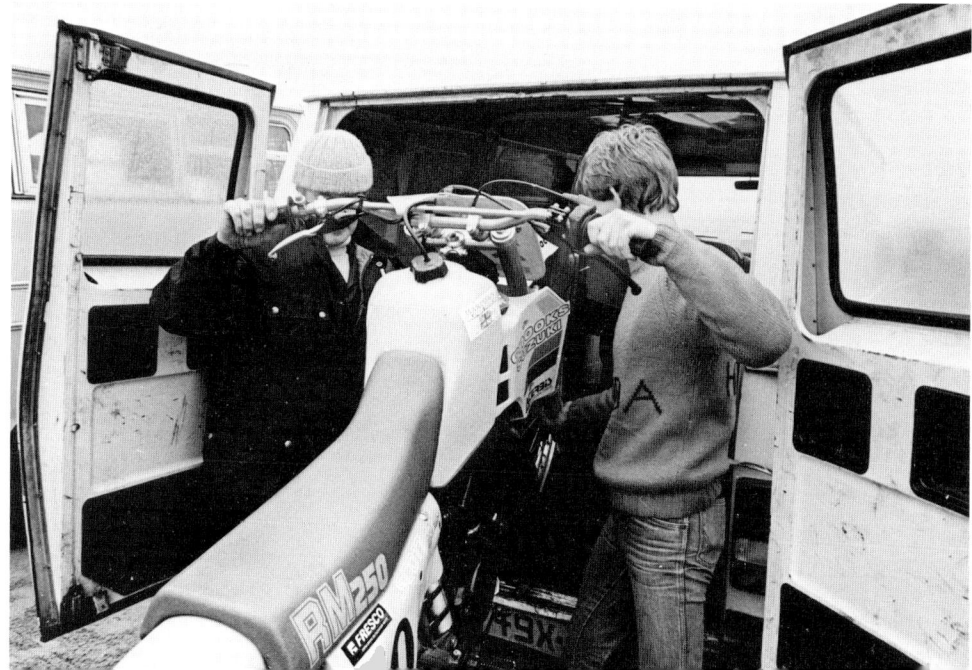

used for long journeys carrying a heavy, static load – for example an unarmoured security van. The worst possible candidates would be a van used on short, stop-and-start trips, carrying bulky items which had to be manhandled all the time: a city centre parcels delivery service would fall into this category.

If a van has been used by a commercial organization, it will have been very heavily worked: you may be sure of this above anything else. Again, considering the example we examined earlier, it is virtually impossible for a van to have done only 7,500 miles in a year except in the exceptional circumstances I described. A more realistic figure would be in excess of 24,000 miles if the vehicle was used by a local company. The reason for this high mileage is simple. The firm's transport manager wants to see his company's investment utilized to its maximum and unless the vehicle is being used almost every hour of every working day, it will be sold as surplus to requirements.

By the time a petrol engine has powered a van for about 60,000 miles, it is getting tired and will want money spent on it so any prospective van purchaser should take this into consideration, remembering of course, that engine life varies dramatically between one van and another. By contrast, a diesel engine will last much longer – 100,000 miles is nothing to one of these power plants. Naturally diesel powered vans are more expensive when they do come on the second-hand market, although they are more economical to run if somewhat less lively in terms of performance than petrol powered vehicles.

Regardless of what type of power unit the van has, the way the vehicle has been driven will be the key factor to its state. Company-owned vehicles will be more likely to have been driven by a pool of drivers, none of whom has specific responsibility for the care and condition of the van and therefore has had no vested interest in looking after it. A vehicle driven by a private individual, or an owner-driver in a small firm, will be far more likely to have been used with courtesy and consideration. Clearly, such a vehicle is well worth a premium price.

*Left:* **Loaded correctly, a bike will take up very little room in a van. Note the author's bike leans away from the wall of the van so that the bike's weight keeps the tie-downs under tension.**

*Below:* **The correct way to locate a front wheel in a van – pointing inwards and tensioned against the door pillar.**

## Trailers

The problem with a van is that for many people it is not a convenient vehicle for every day use. Personally, I enjoy driving a van and I would not mind having a tasty, customised *Transit* for personal transport but often, business or family commitments mean that it is not possible to have a van if this is to be your only vehicle. Running costs too are high with fuel consumption in particular being potentially a major drain on income. The fact that vans are also restricted to 50 mph except on motorways is also an irritant.

The solution is a car and trailer. With this set-up, the car can be used in all its normal rôles from Monday to Saturday and be employed as a towing vehicle on Sunday. For help with this section, I turned to Ches. Gray who is the owner of Warrington Trailer Centre, the North West's biggest independent towing centre and himself a motorcycle fan for many years.

The first problem to clear up is the type of car suitable for towing. This is easily settled in the knowledge that almost any car on the road today will tow a single bike trailer. Whether they do this more or less happily is another matter. Certainly a typical 1300 cc hatchback will haul a bike, trailer and all the gear necessary for racing without any effort at all. The real minis — below a 1,000 cc can do the job but they are going to be struggling.

**The author's custom-built 'flying coffin' trailer. Effortless to tow and load and with a vast carrying capacity.**

Fitting a tow-bar to any car is no problem at all. Warrington Trailer Centre will make a 'bar for any car whatsoever and a search through Yellow Pages will no doubt reveal other specialist manufacturers who will tackle one-off jobs. The only cars Warrington Trailer Centre try to avoid are fibre-glass bodied sports cars which require very complex 'bars to attach to the car's chassis. These jobs can be done, but tend to be expensive. There are many tow-bars on sale and Ches. warns against buying with price as the sole criteria. Cheap tow bars tend to be just that and purchasers should expect poor materials and the liklihood that the tow-bar will not be a good fit on the car. In addition to making his own tow-bars, Ches. recommends *Witter*, *Dixon-Bate*, and *Watling* as all being first-class products.

Apart from your views on what will be a suitable vehicle for towing, the law must influence your decision too. Current British laws are in sympathy with EEC regulations, so it is unlikely that they will be dramatically modified in the near future but it is essential to check the regulations applicable at the time since rules have a habit of changing unexpectedly.

At present, the regulations state that a car cannot tow a vehicle and trailer with a gross weight exceeding 50% of the vehicle's weight. For example, a 1.6 Ford *Sierra* weighs 1020 kg so the maximum weight of trailer and load it can legally tow is 510 kg.

In practice, this poses little restriction for the racing motorcyclists. A typical motocross bike weighs 120 kg complete with fuel. A single bike trailer will weigh about 50 kg. So their combined weights are under a third of the maximum permissible towing weight for a *Sierra*. Even with three bikes, it is unlikely that the maximum towing weight will be exceeded. There is also a useful exemption for trailers under the 750 kg maximum weight limit in that no additional braking system is required, thus avoiding the use of linked brakes, which are expensive and an unwanted complexity.

The law is equally sympathetic regarding lights. Although it would be foolish to build a trailer without lights, if the lights and indicators of the towing vehicle can be seen adequately from **every angle**, there is no legal obligation to have additional lights fitted.

If they are — and all bike trailers should have lights and indicators since even a single bike trailer is too bulky to rely solely on the car's lights to warn following vehicles of its presence — they must duplicate the display at the rear of the car. This means that there must be red rear and stop lights and amber indicators. The lights must be between 350 and 900 mm from the ground and at least 400 mm apart — again, little more than common-sense. Finally, two red reflective warning triangles must be displayed.

One of the great sources of irritation to racers towing trailers has been the imposition of a 50 mph speed limit. Crawling along an empty motorway at 50 mph is mind-numbingly boring and is perhaps one of the most effective means ever invented of persuading motocrossers to buy vans. However, even this imposition might well end soon since there is talk of this law being relaxed to allow "light" trailers, such as those which would be used for carrying a bike — to be towed at 60 mph. This brings trailers virtually in to line with vans regarding speed restrictions and makes them an even more attractive proposition.

Now, let us consider what is involved in taking the average car and converting it for towing. The first step is to fit a reputable make of tow-bar or have one fitted. At the same time, purchase a seven pin lighting plug and wire it to the ISO layout.

This is essential if you ever want to use another trailer since all commercial trailers follow this standard. Again, seek help from a specialist if you are unsure.

All ball hitches are 50 mm and there is not a bad one made. Ensure that high tensile bolts are used to retain it to tow bar. Finally, make sure that a plastic cover is used to cover the ball hitch whenever it is not being used since ball hitches are always greasy and dirty and will invariably attack the leg of your suit just as you are going to the club dinner dance.

Now to the trailer. This can be as simple, or complex, as you desire, and it can be constructed yourself or bought ready-made. Figs 3 and 4 show two of Warrington Trailer's designs which Ches. has kindly let us reproduce as examples of a basic and custom trailer.

Before considering the trailers themselves, let me add a word of caution about building a trailer. I have built a number and I have enjoyed doing so. Approached in this attitude, constructing a trailer can be an excellent winter project but there will not be a great saving in money. To go from bare metal to the finished product takes me about 40 hours — the painting of the chassis and body panels and the sawing of the angle iron by hand both being very time-consuming. Added to this is the cost of buying all the bits and pieces for the trailer at the retail price so the difference between making a trailer and buying one ready made becomes negligible. The key reason for building your own trailer must be for the fun of doing it, and the pleasure of having a "one-off".

**Warrington Trailers' 'economy' model.**

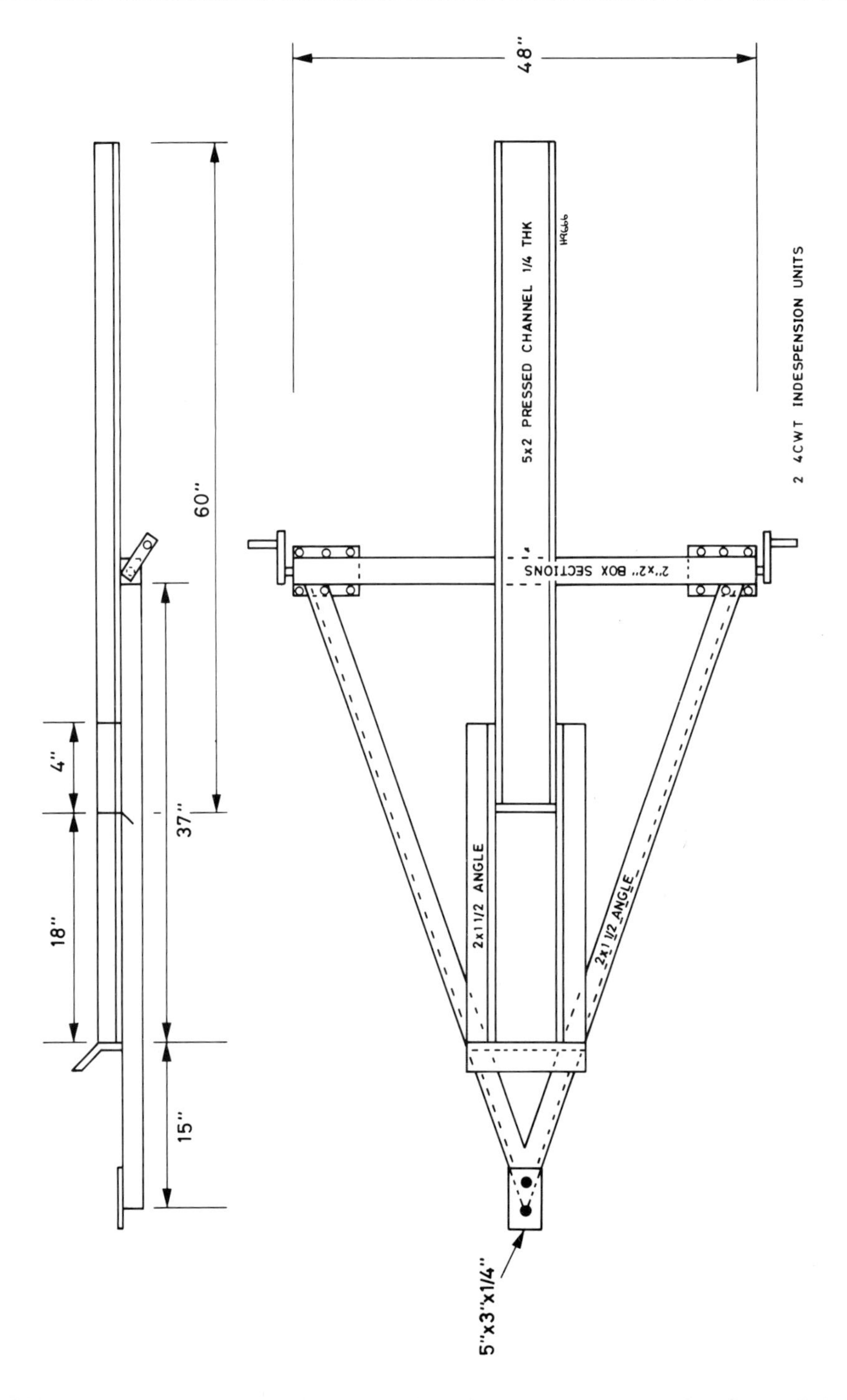

The basic Warrington Trailer design. Fig 8.1

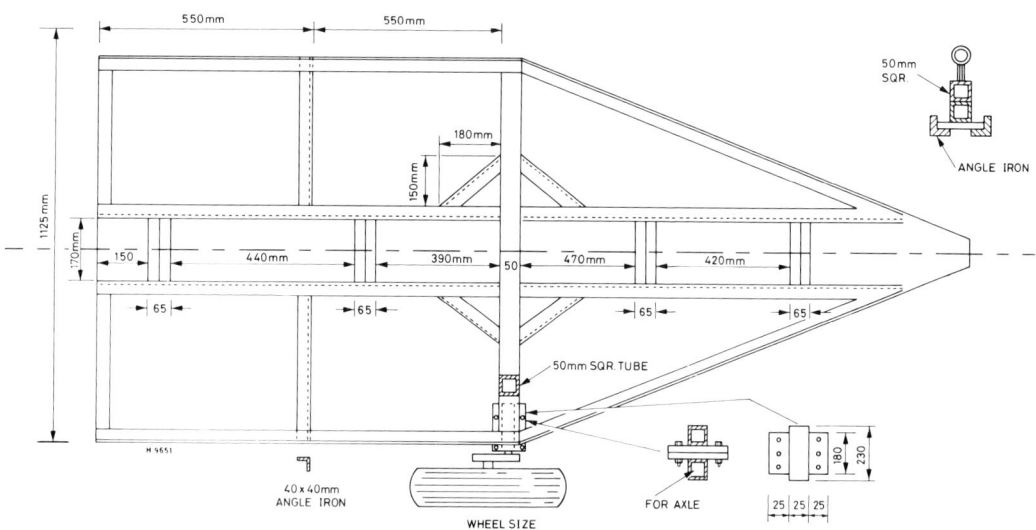

Fig 8.2

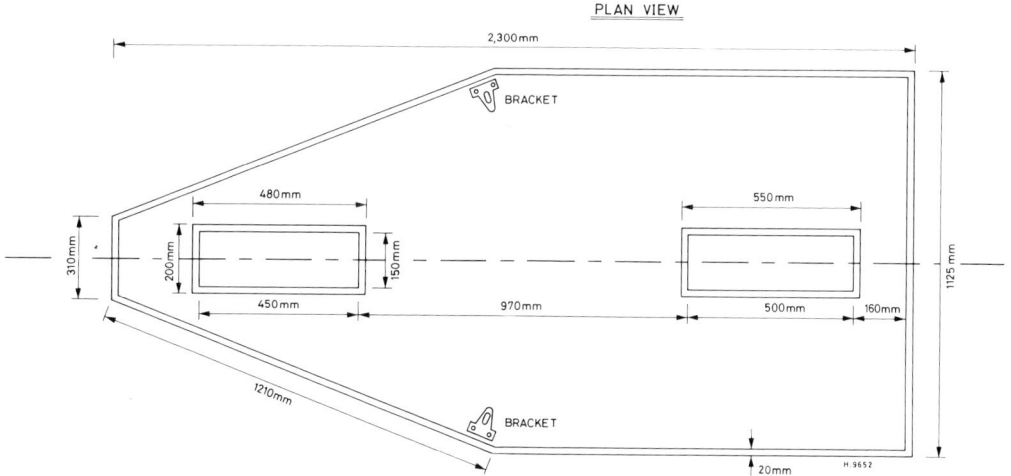

Fig 8.3

**Plans for the construction of a trailer similar to the author's 'flying coffin' design. Figs 8.2 to 8.5**

SIDE ELEVATION

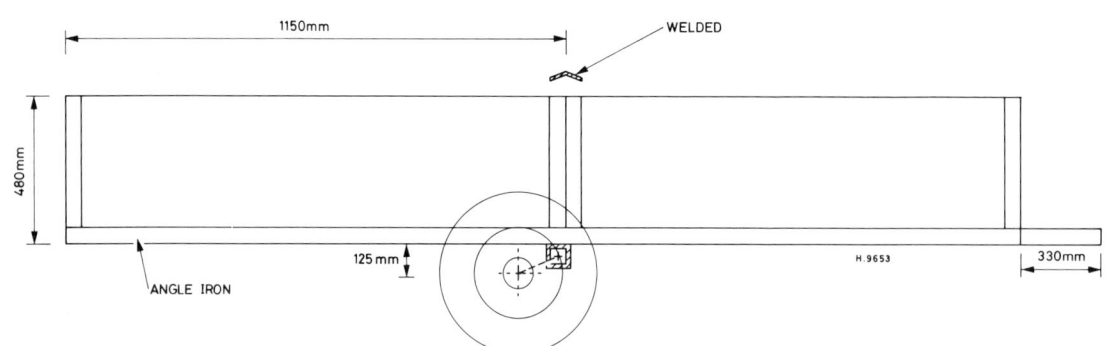

1150mm

WELDED

480mm

125 mm

ANGLE IRON

H.9653

330mm

Fig 8.4

# REAR ELEVATION

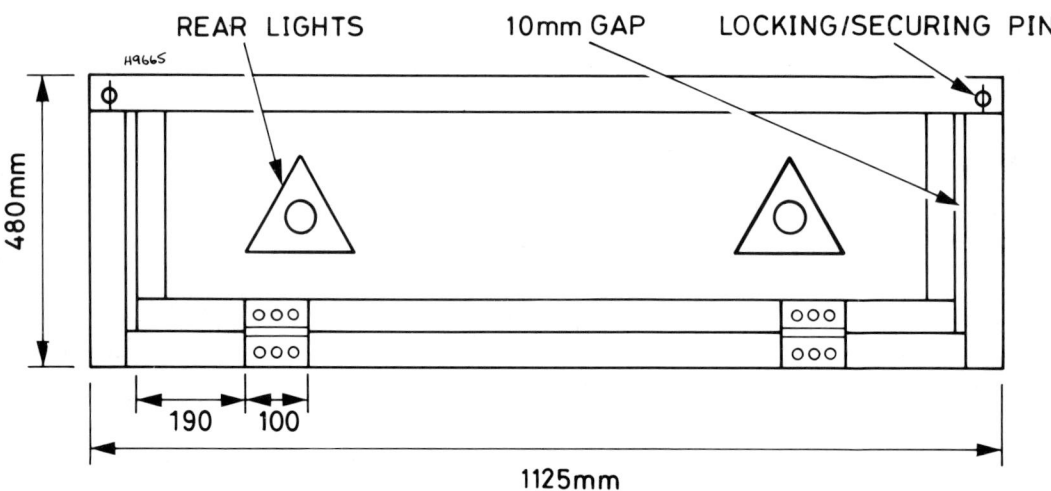

REAR LIGHTS       10mm GAP       LOCKING/SECURING PIN

H966S

480mm

190    100

1125mm

Fig 8.5

In the 'olden' days beautiful hand-made thumpers like this Velocette ruled the world.

The last competitive British four-stroke was the CCM, here being forced along by big John Banks.

Smooth, aggressive and totally unpredictable was Brad Lackey – the only American ever to take the Blue Riband of Motocross: the 500 cc World Championship.

But in 1982, even World Champions worked on their bikes.

. . . and the Japs watch *everything*.

Carla (Hakan Carlqvist) hams it up with the Lumaca dolly birds.

The loneliest place in the world: a G.P. start line.

Legalised warfare! The first turn at the 500 Belgian G.P.

A rear view of first lap tussles at Farleigh Castle in 1985.

Watson uses his patented 'psyching' technique for a first corner lead.

Meanwhile, Vromans gets his head into gear in the same way.

The only problem is that everyone else is doing the same thing.

Go for it!

'Just like the one in the showroom, sir!'. Carlqvist's very special works Yamaha.

'You give it a big handful and then balance on the back wheel!'. Vromans practises speedway on his factory KTM.

In the right hands, 12

Heeled well over. AMCA star Geoff Burton powers his Suzuki through a bend.

Jobe, always neat and effortless in style, is seen here at Namur during the 1985 Belgian Grand Prix.

No dust problems today! Greg Hanson ploughs through the mire at Howe Hills during the 1985 British Championship round.

...n be very spectacular!

Carla, the toughest man in motocross, battles it out at Namur – despite having enough injuries to put a normal man in hospital.

A typical all-action shot of Danny Chandler before he was so tragically injured.

Even teenies can fly!

Even when he doesn't win, Jobe is a very special rider: 40 feet in the air and as relaxed as if he were in the paddock.

G.P. riders never ride – they RACE!!

The dynamic duo. Dave and his dad Keith (one of the best spannermen on the G.P. scene) weigh up the opposition.

Breaking the opposition! Dave prepares for yet another blistering performance in timed training.

The ever-attentive Sharon worries for Dave before the 1984 Italian G.P. She did a good job. Dave won both legs.

A master at work. Thorpey on the way to yet another win, this time before 40,000 Belgian fans.

# A Champion at work

Even under the most intense pressure, Dave is cool and calm.

But he always pulls out the stops in front of his home crowd: Farleigh Castle in 1985.

Not that he suffers when racing on the Continent. Dave won again at the Luxemburg G.P. in 1985.

But wherever he is, Dave is always the complete champion, here being interviewed, photographed and mobbed simultaneously at Howe Hills.

Warrington Trailer's basic single motorcycle trailer is constructed entirely from engineering angle iron – don't be tempted to use bits of old bed or shelving. The axle beam is constructed from 50 mm x 50 mm x 5 mm box section whilst the 'A' frame uses 50 mm x 50 mm x 5 mm angle iron. The trailer spine, in which the bike rests is made from 130 mm x 65 mm x 5 mm channel. This trailer is very simple and tows beautifully but is limited in its uses to towing bikes. With a typical motocross bike loaded on to it, it has a positive weight at the tow of bar of about 30 kg. This is a critical weight. Any more, and the car's suspension will suffer. Much less, and the trailer will snatch at the ball as it lifts over bumps.

By law, all trailers have to be sprung and the only sensible way to achieve this is by using rubber in torsion units. These operate independently on each wheel and are maintenance free, with a very long working life. Again, a number of manufacturers make these but do look for a reputable company with a good history of success in this field.

One final word of warning must be given regarding towing hitches. These are really critical to the whole exercise since they are the bit which joins the trailer to the car! Again, go for quality either in pressed steel or cast-iron, and do make sure that the hitch is bolted to the trailer with high tensile bolts, using self-locking nuts or *Loctite*.

**The correct way to load a motocross bike.**

*Above:* When loading a bike on a trailer, the first tie-down must be put on so that the bike is at an angle. It can then be straightened up by compressing the suspension. The tension from the compressed suspension will keep the tie-downs tight no matter how much the trailer is bounced about.

*Right:* The correct placing of the tie-down. Close to the handlebar clamps to avoid bending the 'bars and with the loose ends secured so that they do not flap about and loosen the tie-downs.

Finally, to the wheels. Warrington Trailer's basic design uses the standard 400 x 8 inch wheel with a four ply tyre designed expressly for trailers. This is perfectly acceptable for a bike trailer and indeed most of my trailers have had these wheels. The problem with them is that because they are so small in diameter the poor things have to fly round to keep up with the much larger car tyres. This difficulty is exacerbated should the driver be tempted to stray above 50 mph. I have seen trailers arrive at meetings which have been driven by some sportingly minded competitor where the wheel bearings have been too hot to touch.

The answer is to go to the 10 inch wheel fitted on *Minis*. This gives the tyres and wheel bearings a much easier life because they rotate much more slowly yet, retain the high-speed taper-bearing hub, specially designed for trailer use. If the speed limit for trailers is raised to 60 mph, the bigger wheels will prove essential.

Fig. 2 shows my own trailer which was built to my specification by Warrington Trailers. It is a de-luxe vehicle in every sense of the word and serves not only as a fine bike trailer but also as a general purpose carrier for the rest of the household. The design is self-explanatory but two points are worth stressing. First there are cutaways for both front and rear wheels of the bike. This means that the bike sits low in the trailer and therefore the centre of gravity is low, despite the use of small diameter trailer wheels.

Second, Ches. took a lot of time in getting the balance absolutely perfect. Loaded or empty, the trailer is always effortless to manoeuvre and there is not the slightest effect on the car's performance or handling. I can even power-slide the car with the trailer in tow — although I would not recommend this trick except off-road and well away from other vehicles!

# Race fit

WHEN I first began racing, it was almost a matter of personal pride that one didn't train or undertake any form of physical exercise. In fact, even this statement is not strictly accurate since for many years, I never actually knew anyone in the motocross world who had any knowledge of, or interest in, physical fitness. Now the situation is very different. Physical fitness is essential not only for the pursuit of race success but also for the rider's safety. Modern bikes are so fast and potentially dangerous that the rider must be strong and agile if he is to ride them successfully.

There are numerous occasions when a skilful rider who is unfit will do better than a superb athlete who cannot ride a bike to save his life. However, this is not a reason for gainsaying the need for physical fitness, no more than the argument that it isn't necessary to have a good bike in order to win races. Rather, a skilful, fit rider, on a well-prepared competitive bike, will prove a very difficult proposition to beat. Remove any one of those factors — skill, machine, or fitness, and the odds on beating him become progressively greater.

In this chapter, we are going to consider the training schedule used by Kurt Nicoll. Kurt is supremely fit as well as being a superb rider and he also enjoys the benefits of first-class machinery. This is why he is usually the first of the non-Japanese factory riders to finish in the Grands Prix!

The schedule gives you some idea of the level a professional rider can work at but don't be too disappointed if you cannot manage it. Remember, Kurt is one of the world's best riders and you won't be able to do what he can achieve on the bike either. Rather, use his training schedule as an ideal towards which you can work and then seek the advice of a trainer at a sports-orientated Health Club or Gymnasium near you for guidance as to at what level you can begin. The silliest, and most dangerous thing to do, would be to try and emulate Kurt's programme from scratch. Not only would you not do it, but torn muscles, strains and other self-inflicted injuries would be sure to arise. For this reason, Kurt has asked me not to quote the weights he used in the gym since what is suitable for him will almost certainly not be suitable for you.

Kurt trains with Liz Hobbs, the Ladies World Water-Ski Speed Champion, and Andy Coe, the European Speed Ski Champion. There is a friendly rivalry between the three and Kurt says this takes a lot of the drudgery out of the training. Undoubtedly, training is more fun and potentially more effective if it is done in groups.

Before any training can be started, the body must be warmed up. Failure to do so will lead to those torn and strained muscles we mentioned earlier. This is Kurt's warming up procedure:

1. Five minutes on the cycling machine.
2. Five minutes over-stretching. i.e. touching toes, stretching legs, trunk curls.
3. Twenty minutes aerobics. Kurt is fortunate in this respect in that Liz Hobbs runs an aerobics school and so can lead the men through this section of the training with ease — even though Kurt is not a world-rated disco dancer!

**Warming up on the cycling machine.**

Then to the programme itself. This is designed to build strength and stamina. Heavy, bulky muscles — such as weight lifters display — would be no use at all to motocrossers, who need agility and stamina as much as strength, so Kurt's trainer, Roy Carter, has designed a training schedule which will give Kurt all these attributes:

1. Two minutes fast cycling. This thoroughly warms the body and also strengthens the quadriceps, or thigh muscles. These are used continuously as the rider goes from a sitting to a standing position on the bike.

2. Two minutes on the rowing machine. Again, this warms the body and also works the biceps, triceps and pectorals.

3. Then to the first of the weight exercises. Kurt does three groups of 15 repetitions, each with a 30 second break between each group. Someone who is not fully fit might be better advised attempting just one set, or taking a much longer break between each group. Take things steadily and do seek professional advice.

4. The first exercise is the shoulder press where the bar is behind the lifter's head and he presses it above his head. This strengthens the shoulder muscles.

**Press for strengthening the shoulder muscles. Exercise 4.**

5. Then to bench presses. Laying down on the bench the weights are pushed away from the athlete. It is advisable to keep the feet on the bench at this time to avoid the back arching and causing damage to the spine.

**Bench presses. Exercise 5.**

6. Now to straddle jumps aside a gym bench. These work the thighs and lower legs but also develop the explosive power necessary if the rider needs to summon extra strength during a race – for example, to force the bike through a section of really rough track to pass the man in front.

7. Then back to the weights with curls to exercise the biceps.

8. Squats taken from the sitting position to standing on tip-toes work both the quadriceps and calf muscles.

9. Leaving the weights for a moment, Kurt goes to sit-ups which follow through all the way until his head touches his knees. Clearly, this exercise strengthens the stomach muscles but the long arc of travel also encourages suppleness in the athlete.

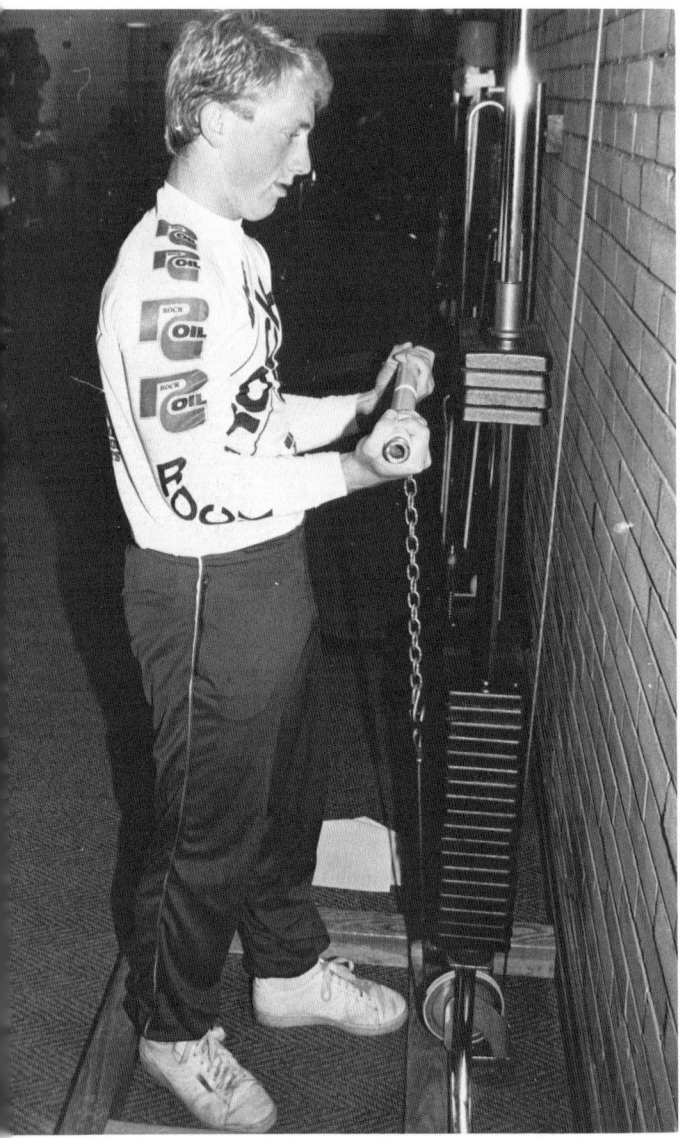

*Above, left:* **'Curls' for the biceps. Exercise 6.**

*Above right:* **Squat thrusts to tip-toes. Exercise 7.**

10. The triceps are strengthened by using weights which are pulled vertically, keeping the arms close to the body so that all the effort is concentrated in the triceps.

11. Sit-ups on a 45° inclined bench give more strength to the stomach muscles and Kurt makes sure the work is sufficient by holding a large medicine ball behind his head at the same time. Again, the exercise is designed to encourage full suppleness since Kurt goes all the way from fully extended to touching his knees with his head.

*Below, left:* **Triceps exercise.**
**Arms are kept close to the body for the best effect. Exercise 10.**

*Below, right:* **Sit-ups on the 45° inclined bench. Exercise 11.**

*Right:* **Exercising the quads through leg extension exercises. Exercise 12.**

*Below:* **Pectoral muscle exercise. Exercise 13.**

12. The quads are worked again through leg extension exercises but there is a great danger of strain with this exercise so take it slowly and carefully and build up to your maximum strength.

13. A return to the weights for a session working the pectoral muscles — those used for controlling the bike in a power-slide — is next.

14. Then the weight machine is used for leg push-ups with a heavy weight to build real strength as well as stamina in the leg muscles.

15. The bench comes back into use when Kurt does press-ups. His feet rest on the bench and then he presses up from the floor with a light weight behind his head for extra emphasis.

*Left:* **Leg push-ups for strength and stamina in the legs. Exercise 14.**

*Below:* **Press-ups off a bench for extra loading. Exercise 15.**

16. To balance the muscle building which has gone on so far, two minutes skipping follows which encourages agility and suppleness.

17. Two minutes bouncing on the trampette provides a break from the hard work and also reduces the build up of lactic acid which leads to muscle fatigue.

18. Next, it is back to building explosive power with 20 metre shuttle runs in which Kurt goes flat out to improve on his previous best time.

19. Then it is to the wall bars for two groups of exercises. First, Kurt hangs from the bars by his arms and lifts his outstretched legs to the horizontal position. The exercise is optimized by attaching light weights to his feet.

20. The second exercise is pull-ups on the bars. As usual, going from a fully extended position so that the muscles' suppleness is maintained.

21. Then it is back to the inclined bench for 3 sets of short, quick pull-ups to build explosive power.

22. Finally, Kurt finishes with three 45 second bursts on the treadmill running flat out.

*Facing page:* **Skipping for agility and balance.**

*Below:* **Three 45 second bursts on the treadmill for explosive power.**

Just as important as gym work is the time Kurt spends running. This can be split into two separate sections. First, what Kurt calls "fun running" in which he covers 4–6 miles every day simply to keep his legs and heart in good working condition and secondly, more serious efforts designed to build explosive power.

After his long run, Kurt concentrates on sprinting and he has a number of exercises which he completes on every visit to the track.

1. Run throughs. These are 60 metre sprints followed by a 15 second recovery period and a further 60 metre sprint and then a 30 second break. Each pair of runs is repeated between ten and fifteen times.

2. These are followed by 100 metre sprints against the clock with the aim of improving on the previous best time during each subsequent run.

3. Finally, Kurt finishes with a series of shuttle runs between 20 metre distanced posts, as carried out in the gym.

In addition to running and gym work, Kurt also works through an individualised programme of weight training designed to build strength. Such a programme must be tailored to the needs of the individual and it is essential to seek expert advice before beginning any weight training. However, as a general guide, Kurt aims at the following ratio of exercises:

1. Three groups of leg exercises.

2. Three groups of arm exercises.

3. One group of stomach exercises.

Given these guidelines, any competent trainer will be able to guide you towards a suitable variety of exercises for your own strength and age.

In weight training, Kurt uses the "pyramid system" where the lifter begins with a relatively light weight and then works progressively towards a peak, finishing by working his way back down to the lightest weight again. The most important difference between Kurt and athletes seeking the ultimate in weight lifting is that he never lifts the maximum weight of which he is capable. Kurt's body is too valuable to risk satisfying a desire to know how good he is when it matters little what he can lift provided he is strong enough to get the winner's trophy over his head at the end of a meeting! If Kurt doesn't need the ego trip, then neither do you. There are enough dangers in racing without adding to them in the gym.

A final part of fitness comes from practice on the bike for perhaps the best training of all is to go riding — it's certainly the most fun! Many G.P. riders argue that you must practice for the length of race in which you are competing. Thus, Dave Thorpe prefers to practice in 50 minute sessions. However, it would seem that this routine is not essential. For example, Broc Glover practises in fierce 6 lap bursts whilst Kurt rides round until he feels he has had enough and then stops. The big danger to avoid is to feel that you have to complete "x" number of laps. This attitude leads to staleness and practising becomes a drudge rather than fun.

It is useful to practice for a similar length of time to that which you will spend racing but a better idea is to try to master the technique which you felt was causing you most problems in last week's race. Get that right and you will feel a sense of satisfaction and purpose from your session as well as enjoying the benefits of physical fitness.

Above all else, never conclude a practice session without putting in two or three laps at your maximum speed. It is all too easy to become accustomed to accepting a slower speed than your best as the norm, and this is an impossible handicap to overcome when racing. So, leave the track with a clear impression of your maximum speed, and you will carry this forward to your next race.

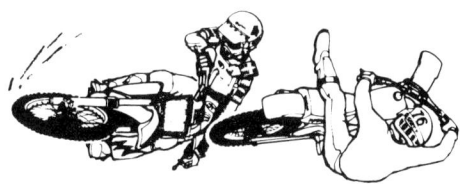

## Motocross injuries

So far in this chapter we have discussed physical fitness. Worthy of careful consideration by every motocross rider it will contribute not only to his speed but also to his safety. However, it must be recognised that motocross is a physical sport and as such involves an element of danger. The chances of getting killed riding motocross are remote but it will be a very lucky rider who does not suffer some injury during his career. This section is to help you recognise the seriousness, or otherwise, of an injury and also to make sense of any comments your doctor may make. It is not intended as a "Teach Yourself Orthopaedic Surgery" course and if there is the slightest doubt in your mind, consult a doctor. Bike bits are available off the shelf: spares for humans are in somewhat shorter supply.

For help with this section, I sought the help of a senior consultant orthopaedic surgeon who has had considerable experience of sporting injuries resulting from football, cricket and motocross. Because of his strict adherence to the ethics of his profession, he refused to accept any public acknowledgement of his invaluable help in the preparation of this part of the book.

The fact that the surgeon concerned is one of the foremost experts in sporting injuries is of the utmost importance, because many doctors tend to view such injuries as self-inflicted – rather like sniffing glue or suffering a bashed head in a drunken brawl. This section of the medical profession will not take kindly to a rider hobbling in with tyre burns all over his leg – even if he was leading the Junior "B" final until his mate on a 250 Suzuki torpedoed him. By contrast, a sports specialist will understand that the injury occurred in the legitimate pursuit of sporting glory and his attitude will almost certainly be more sympathetic.

Equally, the "ordinary" doctor is likely to adopt conservative times for recovery. "Come and see me again in six weeks" is not reassuring if the rider could be back on a bike in safety ten days later – if he were prepared to tolerate more pain that would be acceptable to a "normal" person. A sports doctor will tend to give the minimum resting or recovery time before a rider can compete again without damaging his body. It should be noted that in my experience, sports specialists really do recommend the absolute minimum and if a rider tries to undercut the advice given, he is likely to damage himself and prolong his injuries unnecessarily. The consultant surgeon with whom I worked has seen this happen more than once.

Let us begin by having a look at some of the basic medical terms so that sense can be made of your doctor's comments. First, the fracture. A fracture is the same as a break and means that the bone has parted. Fractures come in a wide variety of

sizes and flavours and range from the almost trivial to the very serious.

The most straightforward are called simple fractures and these are always closed. This means that the bones are contained within their area and do not break clear of the skin. Treatment for such fractures may range from strapping or support at best, to traction or even pinning in bad cases. Clearly, even the simplest fracture needs medical advice.

Much nastier is the compound or open fracture. In this case, the bones are severely displaced and may break clear of the skin. Fortunately this sort of damage is relatively rare for motocrossers and normally will only be sustained when the rider has had a really bad crash, usually when he has been hit by another bike or has collided with an obstacle on the track.

Fractures themselves are caused in two ways: that is, as far as the medical profession is concerned. They do not bother to differentiate between flying over the bars and a belt from behind from a bloke whose girl-friend you have just stolen.

Fractures, or broken bones, can be caused either by a direct blow to the limb as for example, being run over whilst on the ground or alternatively, by hitting the limb or chest wall against a rock, or even hard ground. An alternative way of breaking bones is known as indirect violence. Most commonly this will be caused by very violent twisting such as when a rider catches his foot in a rut at high speed and the leg is turned so hard that the thigh is fractured.

The surgeon stressed that if a rider can remain alert and quick thinking, much damage can be saved by getting his arms and legs as close as possible to his body. The arms should be wrapped round the head which both supports the head and thus reduces the chance of whiplash injury to the neck and also minimises damage to the head itself, arms, elbow and forearm as well as the clavicle, or collar bone. With the elbows pressed tightly against the ribs, then these vulnerable bones will be protected too.

Similarly the legs should be tucked into the stomach and this will do much to protect them. Finally, since the rider hits the ground as a ball, he is far more likely to roll. Injuries always occur when very rapid deceleration happens. If you can slide or roll, then the chances of getting hurt decrease dramatically. Although I have consistently recommended practice in every aspect of motocross, this is one section from which even the keenest competitor may be excused. However, do try and remember this advice should you have the misfortune to part company from your bike.

In addition to reducing the chances of a fracture occurring, other injuries will also be minimised. These fall into three main categories: strains, bruises and dislocations. Again, all these can range from the mildly inconvenient to the very serious.

A strain, as the name implies, occurs when the ligaments which control the body's major movements are stretched unnaturally. At their worst, strained ligaments can be a very real problem since they will lead to a slackness in the joint which may need to be immobilised or corrected surgically.

Bruises are caused by a rupture of the blood vessels or capillaries. The bruising may be deep or superficial. In a superficial bruse, the discoloration will be immediately apparent and the damage more readily assessed. A deep bruise is much more serious in that there could appear to be no damage whilst in fact, a bad injury has been sustained. Medical advice must be sought if a deep bruise is suspected.

Finally, there are dislocations. This type of injury relates to joints which have moved out of their rightful place. The movement is usually caused by indirect violence, like the foot twisting in a rut and as mentioned earlier. Inevitably there is considerable soft tissue damage with straining of the muscles and/or ligaments in the area. The injuries can be fairly straightforward or alternatively can be as serious as a fracture. A sports doctor will give accurate advice on the extent of the damage.

When discussing the question of back and head injuries even this experienced, sports-orientated doctor, was not prepared to comment except to say that all such injuries are potentially very serious and should be treated as such. Immediate advice **must** be sought from a doctor – don't rely on even the most enthusiastic voluntary help at the trackside – although the injury might appear superficially trivial there is not infrequently underlying damage which will require urgent treatment. Never take chances with suspected head or back injuries.

I will conclude this chapter by saying that the surgeon shared completely my enthusiasm for body armour which can help minimise the effects of a crash. He is convinced of the effectiveness of all forms of body protection and the dramatic effect it will have on reducing injuries.

# Joining a club

BEING a member of a motocross club has a rather different meaning to that of any other clubs you may have joined before starting racing. The biggest difference is that you must be in a club to race – it is not an option, like a youth club or the scouts. There are a number of reasons for this compulsion. Some are common-sense and others legal necessities. In the former category is the simple fact that racing is complex to organize. Finding a track, arranging for medical facilities, scrutineering the bikes and buying trophies are all demanding duties and have to be done by someone – they don't just happen automatically! Thus the need for an administrative system.

The second reason for being a club member is for your own safety and more particularly, the strain on your wallet. Every properly organized meeting will have extensive insurance cover. This comes in two quite separate forms. The first, and most important, is third party cover. This means that if your bike flies out of control and hits a spectator – and sadly, this does occasionally happen – the club's insurance will both provide legal representation and also pay any damages which may be awarded. Just to clarify the matter, civil damages these days for a broken arm or leg can amount to tens of thousands of pounds and a barrister's fees will be equally punitive. Clearly, anyone racing without such protection would be insane – a fact which needs remembering when taking part in unofficial practice sessions where spectators are present.

The club will also provide personal accident cover. This varies depending on the organization under whose aegis you are competing. In the case of the AMCA, the rider buys his insurance according to his own requirements whereas the ACU provides standard cover. Neither form will compensate you for lying in a hospital bed whilst your best mate cleans up and steals your girl-friend but at least the insurance money does provide some buffer against lost wages. Neither organization will provide cover against bike damage. However, this is available through specialist brokers although many riders consider it prohibitively expensive. In eighteen years of serious competition, I have never had this last type of insurance cover.

I have already used the terms, ''AMCA'' and ''ACU'' and now I am going to add further to the confusion by introducing the organizations which run youth sport since we will begin by looking at the legal requirements for the youngest riders and then work our way up. First, the youth organizations.

Youth motocross in Britain is organized by three separate groups. By far the biggest is the ACU — short for Auto-Cycle Union. Established in 1907, the ACU runs not only youth motocross events but also trials, grass track and even road racing. ACU clubs also organize the professional events in adult sport such as the British Motocross Championships and also any World Championship rounds which are held in Britain. There are ACU clubs all over Britain and you can be very sure that there will be one near you.

**Racing can be all too much for very young riders.**

Riders in the Nottinghamshire and Derbyshire areas might want to ride with the YMSA, or Youth Motorcycle Sports Association. This club runs trials as well as motocross events and also has some branches in the Devon and Dorset area.

Finally, there is the British Schoolboys Motorcycling Association (also catering for schoolgirls!) which is centred around Swindon and is very active in motocross. Many top riders began their careers with the BSMA.

All three groups have minimum age limits and the engine capacity size of bike a child can ride is also controlled depending on how old he or she is. For example: ACU Juniors can only begin riding when they are seven and they must then ride 60 cc bikes. At the other extreme, YMSA members can continue to compete until they are 21 and they will use 125s. In between, boys and girls will ride first 80 cc bikes and then 100s.

Whilst I am conscious of the desire of many parents to get their off-spring into motocross as soon as possible, I do feel that the dangers of letting a child race too early an age should be considered. Personally, I can see no reason whatsoever to let an eight year old race. Young bodies and minds are not designed for the stresses — both mental and physical — of racing and any parent letting a child of this age race should think long and hard about his or her motives. Does the child want to race or is it more a case of dad or mum using the boy to satisfy their own interests?

If this seems a brutally hard thing to say, it comes from many years of seeing children being encouraged to race at far too young an age and then dropping out of racing when they are 16 or 17 years old, instead of having the time of their life competing all the way until they are a tottering middle-aged wreck like me!

Let a child have a little bike as a toy and do take him to motocross meetings so he gets the taste for the sport, but wait until he is 14 or 15 before allowing him to compete. This is the Belgian approach and their riders seem to fare very well in grand prix racing.

Now to adult sport, which I do most firmly recommend for everyone. This is controlled entirely by the two organisations I have already mentioned, the ACU and the AMCA. As well as promoting professional events, ACU clubs also run motocross events for beginners at club level. These are designated "closed to club" or "closed to centre" meetings. The problem is that whilst ACU clubs are some of the best in the world at running professional events, they are not always as good when it comes to providing sport for the club rider, particularly at entry level. Thus, whilst an AMCA junior will almost certainly be a rank beginner and will not have very much skill at all, an ACU "junior" might be a top-class enduro rider wanting a day's motocross practice or even an ACU expert who has not ridden for a while and has subsequently lost his expert status. A good ACU junior could well compare with an average AMCA expert in terms of riding ability. This means that the novice motocrosser is unlikely to be able to compete against other equally inexperienced riders in his first meetings.

Defenders of the system will argue that is good experience for young riders to race against more proficient competitors, whilst another school of thought suggests that the first-timer is more likely to get depressed at his lack of skill rather than rise to the occasion.

*Facing page:* **Schoolboy racing is fast and spectacular — perhaps too fast and too spectacular for young children.**

I subscribe to the latter view – with one important exception. If you have a lot of schoolboy experience, or you are totally committed to success in motocross, then clearly, the sooner you get tough experience, the quicker the progress you will make. By contrast, if motocross is to be a recreational activity, with success being an added bonus, then the AMCA's carefully graded system of advancement is a much better way of learning the sport.

The AMCA's initials stand for the Amateur Motorcycle Association and their *raison d'etre* is to service the needs of the amateur racer – although never make the mistake of thinking that "amateur" riders are always lacking in skill. Some of the best AMCA "amateurs" are as professional as many ACU experts. Motocross in Britain would be in a very bad state indeed were it not for the AMCA, who run the great majority of club motocross meetings. Equally, the professionalism of the ACU is vital to motocross. The difference stems from the differing needs of the riders each organization has to serve – neither code is "right" or "wrong" and neither is perfect!

ACU riders are very much more on their own than AMCA members and again, this has its advantages and disadvantages. For example, all AMCA members have to attend regular club meetings and have to take part in the organization of events. In fact, every AMCA club has to organize a fixed number of meetings in a year, based on its membership. This is to ensure that the work-load for running events in an area is spread as evenly – and fairly – amongst the riding population as possible. The fact that riders have to attend club meetings is very healthy and means beginners have an excellent opportunity to learn from experienced riders in a social context. They also gain a good insight into the running of motocross and this too, can only be to their benefit.

But there are drawbacks. Because the AMCA's organization is very democratic, pettiness can often creep into club politics as riders unused to wielding any executive power in their normal occupations do so at club level, without considering the wider implications of their actions. On occasions, this is not in the best interests of the riders and can lead to unhappiness. The moral is, carry out some market research on the club you are trying to join before applying for membership. An extra half hour's travel once a month in order to be part of a happy team is a small price to pay for living in harmony.

By contrast, there is no obligation for an ACU member ever to physically go near a club and few ACU riders will be seen attending working parties. Membership of both organizations is obligatory before either one will issue a competition licence but whilst an AMCA club will only grant membership to an active member, ACU clubs will be happy to take a rider's membership fee and never see him. Having said this, there are many ACU clubs with very lively social and organizational elements and who would welcome new faces, so it is vital not to think of ACU organizers as faceless bureaucrats. On the contrary, the great majority are unpaid ex-riders doing a largely thankless job. True heroes indeed!

Having joined a club, you must then decide where to ride. Again, the AMCA will decide for you. You will be told where to ride and in which class you must compete. Your only choice will be that of capacity class. The three AMCA designations for riders are Junior, Senior and Expert. You will begin in the Juniors and depending on your progress, will be moved up the various classes. On the way, you will collect one or two trophies to mark your ever increasing skill. These are very nice to have around and act as an encouragement to do even better in the future.

**Everyone's dream – a full International licence.**

Once qualified as an Expert, there are lots of opportunities for some really exciting activities. First there are the area qualifiers for the AMCA Championships – 125, 250, 750, four-stroke and sidecar. This will provide your first opportunity to ride outside your area. Then there are the Championships themselves which are invariably superbly organized and have all the atmosphere of a really big event. At this level, you can also expect to receive travelling expenses and there will be very few riders racing in AMCA Championships who are not well sponsored by the motorcycle trade since success in this series is considered to be both newsworthy and prestigious. Finally, you could be selected to ride for the AMCA itself in the European Championship (called the IMBA). Riders who achieve this honour have gone a long way past being amateurs and rightly deserve their 'star' status.

However, what is equally as good is to enjoy local racing and perhaps represent your club at an inter-club competition or even do nothing more than travel a few miles to race and have a good Sunday's fun. If these are the limits of your ambitions then be proud of them. Not everyone wants to commit themselves to the expense and sheer hard work of getting to the top in motocross and it is just as laudable – and in many cases much more sensible in terms of time and financial outlay – to do nothing more than race for fun.

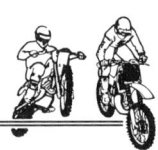

ACU riders have the whole country to choose from when they compete and when I was racing regularly, I enjoyed this freedom tremendously. After making some enquiries regarding a suitable meeting – it will have to be "closed-to-club" or "closed-to-centre" – an entry form is requested from the club. Details of forthcoming meetings are listed in the "Regs Available" section of *Trials and Motocross News*. The form – called regulations but known to everyone as "regs" – will state the venue, the status and organization of the event. All AMCA events follow a fixed pattern but each ACU event is really a one-off and varies tremendously. At this stage, it is a good idea to 'phone the secretary of the meeting and explain that it is your first race and ask him whether the meeting is suitable for a beginner. You will invariably be treated with courtesy and the secretary will no doubt admire your common-sense in asking a sensible question, so don't be shy.

**A typical set of regulations and entry form for a closed-to-club event.**

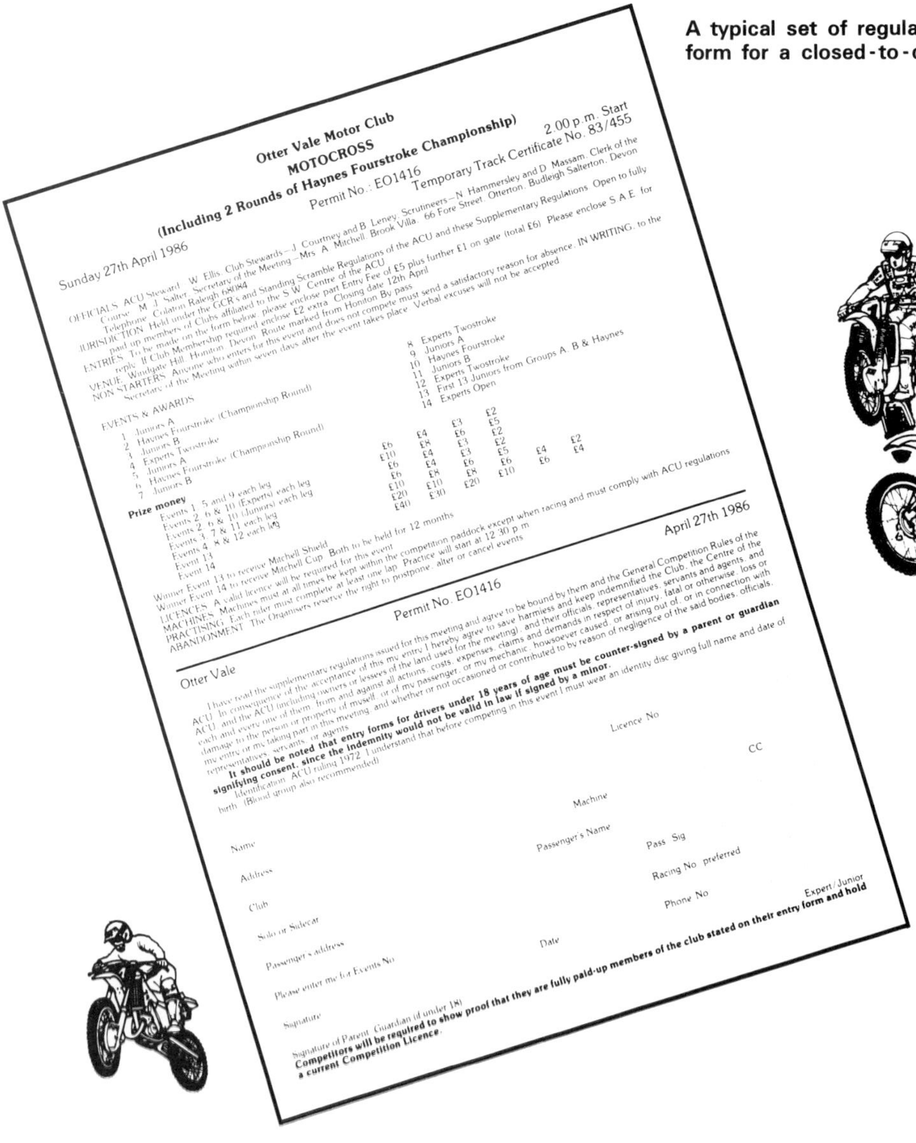

**Otter Vale Motor Club**

**MOTOCROSS**

**(Including 2 Rounds of Haynes Fourstroke Championship)**

Sunday 27th April 1986 Permit No.: EO1416 Temporary Track Certificate No. 83/455 2.00 p.m. Start

OFFICIALS ACU Steward W. Ellis. Club Stewards – J. Courtney and B. Leney. Scrutineers – N. Hammersley and D. Massam. Clerk of the Course M. J. Salter. Secretary of the Meeting – Mrs. A. Mitchell. Brook Villa. 66 Fore Street. Otterton. Budleigh Salterton. Devon Telephone Colaton Raleigh 68084

JURISDICTION Held under the GCR's and Standing Scramble Regulations of the ACU and these Supplementary Regulations. Open to fully paid up members of Clubs affiliated to the S.W. Centre of the ACU

ENTRIES To be made on the form below, please enclose part Entry Fee of £5 plus further £1 on gate (total £6). Please enclose S.A.E. for reply. If Club Membership required enclose £2 extra. Closing date 12th April

VENUE Windgate Hill. Honiton. Devon. Route marked from Honiton By pass

NON STARTERS Anyone who enters for this event and does not compete must send a satisfactory reason for absence, IN WRITING, to the Secretary of the Meeting within seven days after the event takes place. Verbal excuses will not be accepted

EVENTS & AWARDS

1 Juniors A
2 Haynes Fourstroke (Championship Round)
3 Juniors B
4 Experts Twostroke
5 Juniors A
6 Haynes Fourstroke (Championship Round)
7 Juniors B
8 Experts Twostroke
9 Juniors A
10 Haynes Fourstroke
11 Juniors B
12 Experts Twostroke
13 First 13 Juniors from Groups A, B & Haynes
14 Experts Open

**Prize money**

| | | | | | | |
|---|---|---|---|---|---|---|
| Events 1, 5 and 9 each leg | £6 | £4 | £3 | £2 | | |
| Events 2, 6 & 10 (Experts) each leg | £10 | £8 | £6 | £5 | | |
| Events 2, 6 & 10 (Juniors) each leg | £6 | £4 | £3 | £2 | | |
| Events 3, 7 & 11 each leg | £6 | £4 | £3 | £2 | | |
| Events 4, 8 & 12 each leg | £10 | £8 | £6 | £5 | | |
| Event 13 | £20 | £10 | £8 | £6 | £4 | £2 |
| Event 14 | £40 | £30 | £20 | £10 | £6 | £4 |

Winner Event 13 to receive Mitchell Shield
Winner Event 14 to receive Mitchell Cup. Both to be held for 12 months

LICENCES A valid licence will be required for this event

MACHINES Machines must at all times be kept within the competition paddock except when racing and must comply with ACU regulations

PRACTISING Each rider must complete at least one lap. Practice will start at 12.30 p.m.

ABANDONMENT The Organisers reserve the right to postpone, alter or cancel events

Otter Vale Permit No. EO1416 April 27th 1986

I have read the supplementary regulations issued for this meeting and agree to be bound by them and the General Competition Rules of the ACU. In consequence of the acceptance of this my entry I hereby agree to save harmless and keep indemnified the Club, the Centre of the ACU, and the ACU (including owners or lessees of the land used for the meeting), and their officials, representatives, servants and agents, and each and every one of them, from and against all actions, costs, expenses, claims and demands in respect of injury, fatal or otherwise, loss or damage to the person or property of myself, or of my passenger, or my mechanic, howsoever caused, or arising out of, or in connection with my entry or my taking part in this meeting, and whether or not occasioned or contributed to by reason of negligence of the said bodies, officials, representatives, servants, or agents

**It should be noted that entry forms for drivers under 18 years of age must be counter-signed by a parent or guardian signifying consent, since the indemnity would not be valid in law if signed by a minor.**

Identification ACU ruling 1972. I understand that before competing in this event I must wear an identity disc giving full name and date of birth (Blood group also recommended)

Licence No

CC

Machine

Name

Passenger's Name

Pass Sig

Address

Racing No preferred

Club

Phone No

Expert/Junior

Solo or Sidecar

Passenger's address

Date

Please enter me for Events No

Signature

Signature of Parent Guardian (if under 18)

**Competitors will be required to show proof that they are fully paid-up members of the club stated on their entry form and hold a current Competition Licence.**

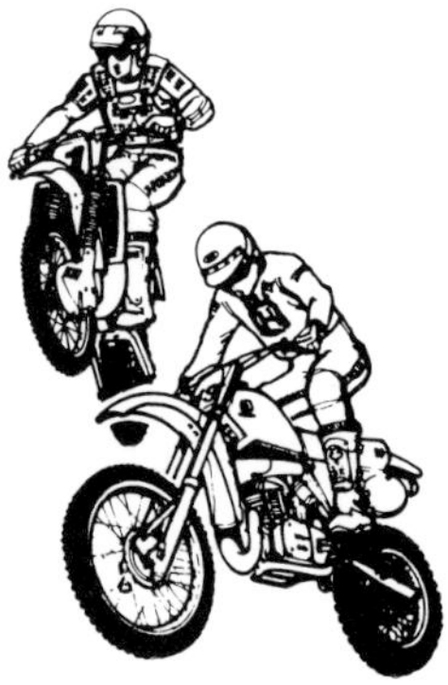

Because there are far fewer ACU events than AMCA, you will have to spend most of your time travelling unless you are lucky enough to have a local track. Even if this is the case, it is unlikely that there will be more than two or three meetings there a year so the situation is not eased to any great extent. Clearly, ACU racing is for the more dedicated rider, or alternatively, the man who wants the occasional outing at a local event.

In each new area where you race, another club will have to be joined. This is in contrast to the AMCA — which might not offer much freedom of choice regarding venues but does require the minimum of formality if you do have to travel. The freedom to race when the where you wish and the lack of compulsion to help with the organization of events both have to be paid for with additional administrative costs in joining clubs and also the punitive financial demands of travelling.

Filling in the entry forms or regs is quite straightforward although the prospect seems to fill many riders with horror. The answer is simply to work through the sections steadily, making sure you fill them all in. At the same time, note the venue. Track locations change — even if they have the same name. I know this all too well having arrived at where the meeting was three months ago only to find that club had moved the track into the next valley. Very embarrassing!

I must conclude this chapter on a serious note. Until a rider is 18 years old, he is not legally an adult — not even if he has won a G.P. This means that all entry forms must be countersigned by the rider's parent or guardian. If you have a job and are a hot-shot racer, the temptation is to do what any man of the world would do and omit trotting off to dad to ask his permission to race. Resist the urge since without your parent's signature, the vital insurance we discussed earlier is invalid. If you do need the support of the insurance companies and you leave them with an escape route, then be assured that they will wash their hands of you. Keep meticulously to the rules and save the risk-taking for the track, where it will pay benefits.

Whichever organization you decide to join — and happily, there is a lot less rivalry between the two than there once was — do try to give as well as take. The old adage really is true regarding motocross: the more you put into the sport the more pleasure you will get out of it.

# Riding techniques

OVER the years, I have been fortunate enough to ride almost all forms of racing motorcycles, from TT-winning production racers to vintage trials bikes. Without any question, the best fun of the whole range has been provided by a motocross bike. Nothing is as agile, responsive or explosively quick as a crisp motocross bike and nothing comes as close to being alive. A motocross bike will go, stop, turn and then stand up on its back wheel for you almost before it's asked. Absolutely the sport of kings!

Because the bike is capable of doing so much so well it deserves to be treated with respect. Handle it carelessly and any decent competition bike will spit you off and probably run over you as well. And this is how it should be. A motocross bike is quite unlike any other motorcycle and whilst you might be the Billy Whizz of the trail bike world, trying to use the same tactics on a racing machine will lead only to a quick meeting with *terra firma*. Instead of applying any knowledge or experience you might have gained on other motorcycles accept that you know nothing and start from the beginning. Other than the controls being in the same place as a trail or road bike, a motocross machine will be completely different. The first ride is better conducted in peace and quiet and let us be clear that at this stage we are discussing riding, not racing. Racing is a separate skill in itself and we will look at this later in detail.

The first step towards racing is to become confident in riding the bike. This sounds almost childishly obvious but watch any motocross meeting and it becomes clear that a substantial minority of the competitors cannot actually ride their bikes. That is, they do not know how to make the bike carry out the basic tasks of acceleration, braking and simple cornering. This is because they began racing before they learnt to ride.

Find a quiet practice track with as few people on it as possible, preferably none. The less distractions around, the greater the chance of becoming familiar with the bike. However, never under any circumstances, practise alone. This is extremely foolish and is potentially lethal. If you use private land, make sure you have the owner's permission.

When sitting on the lowest point of the saddle, the bars should be angled back towards the rider's arms, which should be bent. The handlebar grips should be almost parallel with the ground. Now, with the bike supported, stand up on the footrests, push back until your arms are straight. In this position, the clutch and brake levers should be in a line with your arms. Not so far down so that they are not instantly to hand and avoiding an excessive rise which would mean bending the wrist awkwardly to reach them.

**The correct position for the clutch lever.**

When standing, the rider's feet automatically pivot downwards. Adjust the rear brake lever so that the brake does not bite every time you stand up. At the same time, check that the gear lever is in a comfortable position. If it is adjusted too low, there is chance that it will be nudged when you stand up and if it is too high, lifting the left boot for every gear change will become hard work.

Why the stress on setting the bike up for a standing position? The answer is that the majority of the action takes place on a motocross bike with the rider standing. Most of the time, when seated, the rider's work load is low – except for using the throttle and possibly cornering.

Kick the bike up and set off for a gentle lap. Get into the standing position as soon as possible and feel the bike work beneath you. Notice how the front end of the bike becomes light as weight is moved to the rear. This is the first important

The correct position for the rear brake pedal.

The author demonstrating the 'attack' position used for dealing with most bumps on a motocross track.

lesson. Where the rider's weight is positioned on the bike dramatically alters the centre of gravity and therefore the handling.

On most bikes today, merely opening the throttle will cause the front wheel to lift. Start playing with this since it is a key skill to master. Tweak the throttle and the front wheel will lift, snap it closed and it will descend instantly. Good fun can be had by trying to keep the front wheel up as long as possible whilst maintaining a standing position. Notice that if you lean back, the bike is much more inclined to wheelie. Conversely, when leaning forward, it tends to stick to the ground. This is a vital lesson to learn. Note also that if you are too far back, the wheelie becomes unpleasant and uncontrollable with a distinct chance of the bike flipping over. To correct this, the throttle has to be shut and weight transferred forward. Learn to recognise a severe wheelie in its early stages since in a race, the last thing which any racers wants is to have to close the throttle.

When you are confident of instigating and correcting a wheelie standing up, try the same exercise sitting down. This is much harder to do and requires much finer throttle control since correct weight movements are harder to make. Remember what we said initially. Most of the action on a motocross bike is carried out

**When climbing hills, the rider's weight should be transferred forward to prevent excessive front-end lightness.**

**Weight should be moved rearwards for descents. This reduces the loading on the front forks and gives them a chance to work effectively.**

standing up. Watch a rider who is seated go quickly and you may be sure he has considerable quality.

Having established that weight transfer is critical, let us expand that idea of finding drive. At one time, traction was of critical importance to every motocross rider since on the old bikes no-one could ever find adequate drive. Now, with the advent of rising-rate, long travel rear suspension, it is rarely a problem except in extremely adverse conditions — usually snow or mud. The more weight there is over the back then the better the traction will be. However, don't forget that when drive is found, the front end will be very light. So, if drive is difficult to find, get your weight back over the rear — this time, preferably with your bum on the saddle.

Too much drive is often as much of a problem as too little. Again, body weight holds the key. Naturally, to lose drive, body weight must be moved forward. This time a further interesting phenomenon occurs. Not only does the rear wheel lose traction but the front gains it. The most accurate and reliable steering comes with having plenty of weight over the front end. This is why riders can be seen sliding right up over their saddle on to the petrol tank in corners. It is to make the front wheel steer more accurately. Practise exploring how different body positions can affect the bike's behaviour on the same corner.

Another door is opened with the loss of drive: the bike can now be slid around a corner. This technique is called power-sliding and it is a means of turning the bike very quickly by stepping the rear end out — rather like a speedway rider.

Again, in its simplest form the trick is easy to perform. Slide well forward on the bike until the petrol tank is well between your legs and turn into a gentle corner using first or second gear. Don't worry about speed since no-one is asking for any heroics at this stage. Open the throttle smartly and the rear wheel will step out in the opposite direction as the corner. That is, if the bend is a left-hander the rear wheel will move smartly to the right. To correct this and bring the front and back wheel into line, turn the handlebars against the corner — in the case of a left-hand bend, to the right. Like wheelieing, practise this skill on flat, hard ground where there is a lack of traction. This is the easiest form of terrain on which to learn.

**Apply power and the rear wheel steps out.**

When you can pitch the bike into a corner at forty-five degrees to the track, hold the power-slide with the front wheel two feet in the air and adjust your goggles at the same time, you may be satisfied that you have mastered this skill. The previous description, by the way, is of Hakan Carlqvist in action — probably the greatest exponent of power-sliding motocross has ever seen.

Now that we have established that the front wheel can be lifted by both throttle and body movement let us consider a practical application of this skill. All motocross tracks are rough and to deal with the bumps, the front forks have to be fully extended, so that all their travel is available to soak up the undulations. So, when crossing bumps stand up and get the weight well back and at the same time keep the throttle open.

Turn the 'bars into the slide and roll off the throttle. The bike straightens out automatically.

Power-sliding the bike. Weight well forward to make the front wheel 'stick' and also to lighten the rear wheel for ease of control. The foot is used on the inside of the bend for balance and support.

**If you don't correct the slide then . . .**

This is where thoughtful practise becomes so valuable. A surprising number of riders do not appreciate the need to tackle bumps with power on. The more severe the bumps then the firmer this rule must be applied. The reason for their failure to comprehend is that they cannot manage to keep the engine revving in the what would be the ideal gear for the speed at which they are travelling. The wise rider appreciates that there must be power to that back wheel and drops down a gear so that the same speed is maintained but at higher engine revs. Meanwhile, the Noddy rolls off the throttle, the forks dip causing the back end to kick-up and in a trice the rider has given up motocross and transferred his allegiance to flying —albeit for a relatively short period. A golden rule is that bikes always behave better under power and are at their most dangerous coasting.

The next area where weight transfer plays a major role is in braking. The majority of the braking on any bike should done with the front brake. This maxim is particularly valid for motocross where the major purpose of the rear brake is to steady the bike — unless of course, you are a G.P. rider who needs every last millimetre of brake area to stop. However, at this stage let us assume that your needs are less demanding.

Clearly, as the front brake is applied, the forks will dip, robbing the rider of that precious travel. The answer will be obvious by now: get the weight to the rear of the bike. This time, the arms will have to be locked against the braking force which is quite severe. Braking and steering the bike at the same time will quickly begin to tax the arms and provide a worthwhile reminder that training pays dividends.

Always use both brakes together and now the reason for setting the rear brake up in the standing position can be seen. Too much play under the right boot will

make the brake impossible to apply accurately, whilst too little will mean that it is inadvertently used every time the rider stands. Braking is a key skill and yet another one which few riders really master. The front brake lever should be set so that the brake is fully on about 35mm from the handlebar. This might seem quite close but there is a reason for this. The hand is at its most powerful – and sensitive – when it is nearly closed. Set the brake lever too far away from the handlebars and braking becomes too difficult and lacks feel.

Top-class riders use all four fingers for braking and only touch the anchors when there is a pressing need to decelerate: they really hit them hard! For example, Kawasaki ace Laurence Spence was wearing out a set of disc pads and a pair of brake linings during EVERY race at the dry G.P.s during the 1984 season.

Personally, I have never been strong enough to take all four fingers from the bars so I use the first two digits for most of the race and employ four only in panic situations. Initially, try with two fingers and then progress to four.

Practise braking hard until the front wheel locks and begins to slide to one side. Immediately the brake is released, the bike's steering geometry will straighten out. Continue doing this until you ride two or three metres with the front wheel locked. Mastery of this skill is essential since when braking under racing conditions, it is inevitable that the wheel will lock. Having practised straightening out the slide, you will be confident in your ability to do it again. In fact, the correction will be automatic. Riders who haven't mastered this skill join the earth-sniffing club.

The same skill should be perfected for rear wheel braking except in this case the slide which results from locking the rear wheel is corrected in the same way as a power-slide: by turning the 'bars into the slide. This is a much easier task than sorting out a wayward front wheel.

Finally, we come to the most spectacular part of motocross – jumping. At one time, this was a very clever thing to do which required a lot of skill and thought. Now, with current suspension, it is much easier and bikes are infinitely more forgiving of rider error. For example, not so very long ago, a front wheel landing always led to a crash. Now, front forks are so good that they mask the mistake. Even so, the fact that the bike will cover your errors does not make it any the more pardonable. The rules for jumping haven't changed whether they be a one metre skip down a bank or a 30 metre flight over a table top jump. The key maxim is that there must be power to the back wheel on take-off. Thinking back to how we dealt with bumps, you will remember that in some circumstances, it will be impossible to have the bike accelerating hard in the ideal gear so we maintained the same speed by using more engine revs. and a lower gear.

The same applies to jumps. Make sure that the engine is pulling well over a jump regardless of the actual take-off speed. Launch yourself with the engine shut-off and the bike will flop about like a wounded penguin. There are a few circumstances when a jump is tackled with throttle closed but these are advanced riding techniques which we will discuss in detail in a later chapter.

The easiest jumps of all are those artificial ones constructed on straights. The main problem which faces the rider is psychological plus possibly the strength

*Facing page:* **You must be able to brake straight, true and hard. Note the front forks are depressed but still working effectively because the rider's weight is to the rear. The clutch is withdrawn at the last moment to prevent the engine stalling and also to get it back instantly into the power band when braking is finished.**

required in dealing with the landing if the track is very rough. Take off with power on and the bike will fly itself through the air and land without any rider input. Let us consider why this is.

You will remember that if we needed to wheelie the bike, we stood up, transferred the weight to the rear of the bike and applied power. A jump is just like an extended wheelie with the rear wheel clear of the ground. The bike will fly through the air with the front wheel slightly higher than the rear. Once airborne, close the throttle to stop the engine over- revving. This will have the secondary effect of making the motor act as a brake when landing thus causing the front wheel to come to earth. As I said earlier, the rider is almost an irrelevance.

Landings should always be rear wheel first. The front end will come to earth automatically and the rider's legs will absorb the shock of landing. Immediately the front wheel is on the ground, the rider can assume the sitting position and nail the throttle again.

**The classic jump. Almost automatic on a modern bike.**

Jumping uphill is very similar. The only problem here is that too much power applied on take- off could cause the bike to flip over. The initial "wheelie" would be too severe. Again, weight transference is the answer. Get the weight well forward so that the bike assumes a flatter flight profile than the basic jump. This stance also puts the rider in the correct position for keeping the front end of the bike down under acceleration up the hill. When the second jump is completed, we want full power to be applied but we can't do this on a hill without danger of

**For downhill jumping the rider's weight should not be too far back.**

the bike flipping over. So maintain that weight forward stance on landing to keep the front end down and then get the power on hard.

Finally, the downhill jump. Not unexpectedly, this is the reverse of the uphill jump. Unless the rider is a real expert, this is one manoeuvre which does **demand** a rear wheel landing. Land on the front wheel downhill and the chances are that the bike will pivot round the front end, sending the rider on low flying lessons.

So, once again, plenty of power on take-off. This time, get the weight well to rear to lighten the front end and guarantee the rear wheel hitting the deck first. Keep the weight well back for landing since the closed throttle will tend to bring the front wheel down quickly and we don't want it to crash to earth. Rearward placed weight will slow down the return to earth and make the landing smooth and controlled. These are the two key words: smooth and controlled. The easier you can make the job then the quicker the power can be screwed back on. This point is often forgotten by amateur riders. Jumps are wasted time! The sooner the rear wheel can be got back into contact with the ground and the throttle opened, then the quicker the bike will go. Jumping is little more than a spectacular form of having a rest between the real racing which is done on the track.

Before actual competition is considered, master all these basic skills. Make sure that you can turn the bike using a berm or a power-slide; that jumping holds no fear for you and most of all, that you can brake really hard.

Now, we're ready to put these skills into action with some serious racing techniques taught by some of the world's best riders, including 500 cc World Champion, Dave Thorpe. They will show you that all of the "unbreakable" rules I have given you can, and are, likely to be changed all the time – providing you know what you are doing.

# Ready to race

SO now the great moment is almost at hand. The hours spent in the workshop have guaranteed a reliable bike and the self-inflicted exertions of the gym should have ensured an equally well-tuned body. Entry forms have been completed and the licence is all in order. The crowning glory is the receipt of a racing number. Treasure this — you will never have a more memorable one even if you race for twenty years. Now, all that remains is to get from home to the meeting and enjoy the racing.

This exercise can prove either a real trauma or as easy as brushing your teeth, and is a time when the excitement really builds up. For me, after many years of racing, it is still a mixture of the two. Let's see how we can maximise the fun and reduce the aggravation.

There is one golden rule regarding this exercise: no matter how long it takes the night before, get everything ready **then**. If you leave your packing until the morning of the meeting, it is an absolute certainty that you will forget something vital. So, even if it means a late night before the race, persevere so that you can just disappear in the morning with nothing on your mind except racing.

There has to be a compromise between what items are taken and what are left at home. The easiest way to differentiate between the two is to ask a simple and obvious question; can I reasonably expect to use everything I intend taking to the meeting?

The most difficult choice lies in tools and spares so what goes in the van depends not only on the rider's mechanical ability but also his inclination. For example, I have a set of miniature welding bottles and I am a reasonably proficient welder. However, the thought of setting to and welding bits of my bike at a meeting no longer interests me. When I was ultra-keen, I might have been prepared to haul these about but now, if I bend something so heavily that it requires the use of a welding torch to repair the damage, it can wait until the following day. By contrast, no serious G.P. rider would ever be seen without his welding gear: it is just a matter of intent and attitude.

All the tools used for bike maintenance must go, along with a sensible number of spares. By "sensible", I mean such items as a spare clutch and front brake levers, spare cables and inner tubes. All these items are likely to be used and all can be replaced quickly and easily between races. Imagine how you would feel breaking a clutch lever in a 3 mph practice crash and then not being able to race for the rest of the day for the lack of a spare!

It is also wise to take along any service tools you might have. For example, if a puller is needed for the generator rotor, then it is well worth popping this in the tool box, along with a dial gauge. Timing can be set at the trackside in ten minutes. By contrast, I wouldn't bother with gearbox spares. A sick gearbox tends not to respond to five minutes' care and attention in the paddock.

I like to take three boxes to meetings both for ease of use and transportation. The first box contains my tools. These are organized strictly into compartments and I can go instantly to the tool I need because I know just where it is. My tool box is also meticulously clean and contains no extraneous junk. Although I am now proud of my toolbox, I am not snobbish about it since for many years I had the traditional racer's "tool-bin". In this waste container were not only my very expensive and valuable tools but also anything else that was remotely connected with bikes. The result was really a squalid and heavy, pot pourri of grease, mud, junk and tools in which it was always a struggle to find anything. Then I went to the TT races and saw a German mechanic working on his riders' sidecar outfit.

**Ready to race. The author's giant kit bag and three boxes.**

They were in a desperate rush to get the bike ready for practice but the spanner-man always wiped the tool he had used and returned it to its proper place. After ten minutes I realised that he never once had to search for anything and although apparently fussy, he was in fact, about twenty times faster than I would have been since he never once paused to find a tool. He knew where it was without looking.

Work out your own system and then stick to it. As well as looking professional, it might mean the difference between being able to sort out a problem before the next race or seeing the field disappear whilst you ferret around after that elusive 14 mm ring spanner.

In the second box goes implements rather than tools. These are things which are either too big, too bulky, or too dirty to go with my proper tools. Amongst these are the foot-pump, the tyre levers, spare inner tubes, a giant ex-W.D. ring spanner which I reserve not for unscrewing nuts but rather for straightening out bent bars, footrests, and sub-frames. The replacement cables also live in here. Modern cables never break even under the most severe crashes except when the rider fails to bring a spare. Immediately the bike learns that there is no spare, it will deliberately break a cable just to teach you a lesson. Best to bring a couple of spares so that they won't be needed. The implement box also contains clean rags and a roll of duct tape — the latter being too bulky to go into the tool box.

The final box has come into being in more recent years. This contains my lubricants. Now that everything is in aerosol form, it is a good idea to keep these separate, not only for their own protection, but also for the good of everything else. Probably the best definition of a mess is that which can be found in a van after someone has rested the tool box lid on top of a tin of chain lube. After one such accident, rust is never a problem!

Again to save space, all a rider's lubricants need not be taken to a meeting. Chain lube is essential as is contact cleaner and a water-proofing spray. Although Rock Oil will probably shoot me for saying this, the only other oil which is needed is a two-stroke oil. Rock's *K2* will, at a push, lubricate the gearbox sufficiently well for one or two races and will also oil an air-filter or lube a stuck footrest. I feel sure most of the other top specification engine oils can also be pressed into service like this. So, one litre of oil will do three jobs at a minimum.

The next group of equipment to consider is riding gear. As with tools, follow the same rules. If it might be used, take it. If it won't, leave it at home. Clearly, a spare helmet — if the rider is lucky enough to own two — will be wasting space, but two race shirts so that racing can be started fresh and clean after a muddy practice is a pleasant luxury. Having said that, I raced in one shirt for many years for the very good reason that I didn't possess two and I don't remember suffering greatly as a result.

Do take as many goggles as you have and make sure that you do have at least one spare set. Goggles are as important as a helmet and any rider who does not have a spare pair should not race. Broken arms and legs mend — with a bit of patience: eyes don't!

Finally, always take your wet weather gear — even in the middle of a heat wave. The "broken cable rule" applies here. If you don't bring wet weather gear, it is certain to rain and that spoils everyone's racing. So store it at the back of your van and then it won't need to be used.

The amount of riding gear a racer needs is quite astonishing and containing it can be hard work. A nice Christmas present is one of the large kit bags such as the ones made by Clover or M. Robert. Since Father Christmas no longer visits me, I had to buy a bag and a friend of mine got me a plain but very capacious container designed to hold a hang-glider wing. This is extremely strong and is also a size bigger than the normal kit bag, as well as being cheaper. If you do see any hang-gliding enthusiasts — and they are not on the way to hospital — ask them about a wing bag.

It is also worth raiding mum's kitchen for three of four bin liners. After a muddy meeting, these are essential since some riding gear will be just grimy and sweaty and can go into your kit bag whilst other items will need to be placed in isolation. Again, this strategy keeps the van tidy and will also save a lot of work for the following week-end.

Remember that you won't be racing all day and that a motocross meeting can be a cold and uncomfortable place in the wrong weather. Some warm clothing will be needed which can be worn over the top of your riding gear between races. For example, a loose fitting anorak or donkey jacket. It is a good idea to have a woolly hat as well since colds are easily caught when the rider starts wandering around a freezing cold paddock with his head steaming as if it had just come out of a Turkish bath. The only item of clothing which probably won't be changed for racing is your under-pants. After a meeting, these will be sodden and a positive health hazard. The drive home is a lot more comfortable in dry undies!

After clothing, we come to legal requirements. What paper work do we need to race? First is a current competition licence. This is essential regardless of whether the meeting is held under the auspices of the ACU or the AMCA. Then there is the confirmation of entry, again very similar regardless of the governing body. However ACU riders will change their riding numbers almost every meeting so it is as well to make sure that your riding number as issued by the club matches the number on your bike.

With the confirmation of entry will come directions to the venue. These will vary in quality from superb to so vague that they would be challenging for an SAS map-reading team. But they will be all you have so treasure them. As I said in the chapter on joining a club, venues do change — even when the track has the same name — so check on the map that the event really is being held where you think it ought to be.

**Even stars have to have their bikes scrutineered. Here, Jean-Marie presents Andre Malherbe's bike for inspection.**

It is with some embarrassment that I write the next section, having enjoyed an unsullied reputation for lateness this last twenty years. However, skidding into a meeting at the last milli-second is not the best way of going racing. Leave yourself plenty of time for travelling and you will arrive in a much more relaxed and positive frame of mind. My method of timing arrivals to the deadline, plus 30 seconds, is really only suitable if you enjoy the tension of pin-point map-reading and ISDE standard time keeping. It is not really a sensible way to conduct oneself.

The last items to be packed which we should consider are those that look after the inner man – and the inner man's mind. Racing is strenuous and a long day can lead to headaches so do bring your favourite pain-killer. With luck, she will also clean your goggles as well! A simple first aid kit is also very handy. There will be first aid available at the meeting but I am always reluctant to pester the hard-pressed St. John's volunteers if I can deal with the problem myself. In the kit will go the obvious things like plasters and some disinfectant, as well as Optrex, or an equivalent, to wash out the dust which has infiltrated past your goggles. Also, include some crepe bandages to strap any strains or bruises. Such medicaments are all the more essential if you have to drive home at the end of the meeting rather than having a chauffeur.

A primary source of headaches at meetings is dehydration so take lots of liquid. The best way to relieve thirst is by drinking pure, unadulterated water, or water containing one of the new "athletic" brews. The absolute minimum a racer will need to drink to replace moisture lost by perspiration on a cool day is one litre. On a hot day, this figure can be trebled or even quadrupled. So take plenty of water and drink it.

Only a total fool would drink anything alcoholic on a race day. Not only would the rider concerned deserve driving into the ground with a post bumper for the potential danger his intoxication might cause other riders, but he will also stand an excellent chance of injuring himself. As an added bonus, all alcohol causes dehydration in addition to that already incurred through severe exercise.

Do remember to be polite to the lady in your life for as well as consuming water, racing burns up vast quantities of energy. This causes ravenous hunger which can be satisfied by hundreds of thick butties, Mars bars, cake and hamburgers. All this is well-known as fact amongst the racing fraternity. There is, however, an interesting conundrum. During the meeting itself, you may not feel very much like eating. This is due to the generation of nor adrenalin – the body's own stimulant which gets you ready for battle – and suppresses appetite. Incidentally, the same adrenalin also encourages bladder and bowel action which may help you to understand two other well-known phenomena amongst racers. However, once the meeting is over, the adrenalin dissipates and then the body signals that it is vitally short of energy to replace that which has been burnt during the day. Hence the familiar sight of homeward bound racers gnawing on the back legs of bullocks or staggering from mobile chip shops with quintuple curried chips and sausage. The answer of course, is to add a fourth box to the three containing spares for the bikes and in this one, put the vital supplies for yourself and your travelling companion.

Having left ample time to get to the meeting, you will arrive relaxed and ready to race. However, there is work to be done before the story swapping and posing can begin.

The first job is to choose a suitable place to park and this is not as straightforward as it might seem upon first consideration. Personal tastes vary and clearly these will influence you. For example, some riders like to be near the centre of action and park next to the track. Personally, I don't approve of getting my vehicle covered in clag or buried beneath a layer of dust so I like a quiet spot, well away from the track. However, disregarding personal preferences, there are some guidelines which always hold true.

First and foremost, remember that it is always easier to get in to a track than it is to get out. In practice, this means that if you park at the bottom of a steep, grassy hill, and it rains during the course of the event, you will never get out until the farmer comes and charges you a fiver for the privilege of ripping the front off your *Transit* as he drags you sideways up the bank with his Massey-Ferguson. Always park at the top of the hill so if the worst comes to the worst, you can always slide down to the exit.

Secondly, remember that power-washers are now popular and their water runs downhill, just like all other liquids. Again, a good reason for parking on top of the slope.

That power-washer water has to go somewhere! In this case it is down to the vans below.

Third, note the wind direction. Wind blows dust and with a little thought, it is often possible to park uphill and upwind. If you can achieve this double distinction early in your career, then you will be doing really well.

Fourth, try to avoid parking in the middle of the paddock. The same laws which ensure that it will always rain when you don't have an oversuit, and the cable you leave at home will be the one which breaks, will also mean that the one occasion in the year when the bike seizes and you want to go home will be the time when you are totally blocked in by other vehicles. Parking with a hedge on one side means that at least there is some chance of manoeuvre with only a single line of vehicles as obstructions.

With a suitable base established, the bike can be unloaded and presented for scrutineering. It is now that the benefits of having prepared your machine at home become apparent, for without doubt, there will some riders feverishly fettling their bikes even at this late stage — a sure sign not only of inadequate preparation but also of a distracted start to the day's racing.

The author signing on — an essential task before racing can begin.

**Dave Thorpe and Kurt Nicoll walk the track and discuss the racing line together.**

Scrutineering is an essential part of racing. The bike is presented to a machine examiner who checks it for safety. Regardless of how competent the person is who has prepared the bike, there is always a chance that he will have missed some vital check which could end in disaster. I think my own preparation is as good as anyone's and yet I have brought a bike to be scrutineered with the rear wheel nuts loose. Just at the moment of finishing the job, I was called to take a 'phone call and when I returned I started on the next job to be done. This is why professional mechanics will never answer the 'phone when they are involved in the preparation work. An understandable error but a potentially dangerous one.

Remember that the scrutineer is on your side and if he sends you back to correct a fault it is for your safety and that of the rest of the riders. Listen to what he has to say and accept his comments in good part.

After scrutineering, the rider will "sign on". This is not a supplementary dole payment given by a grateful government to help your racing but rather to register your presence at the meeting. It helps the organizers and it also helps you since until you have signed on as being present, your insurance is not valid. Incidentally, competing on a bike which has not been passed by the scrutineer also invalidates your insurance and should you hurt another rider or spectator, the insurance company will throw you to the wolves. And quite right too!

After scrutineering, there will be time to walk the track before practice begins. This is a time for a laugh and joke with your mates but it also has a serious purpose: you should be constructing a racing line in your mind.

Around every track, there is an optimum path which will enable a rider to go as quickly as possible. This is known as the racing line. The route may be the shortest way around a track, or the smoothest, but it is usually a thoughtful combination of the two. There are a number of different racing lines round any track and these will not be the same for every rider. For example, an expert rider might be able to jump the whole length of a downhill section whilst a Junior could only manage to jump the first part and then ride the remainder. Alternatively, a very strong rider could force his bike through an extremely rough section whilst his less fit opponent will take a wider, smoother line. Your job is to work out the best line for you.

This is very easy for me to write, but fortunately I can still remember how every bit of the track looked the same to me when I started, so do what I did. Tag along with an experienced rider — not necessarily an expert — and ask him to show you his line. It won't be very long before you begin to relate your own riding ability to the track conditions and your bike and combine them to make your own decisions about the fastest way round.

When you have mastered this first stage, the second part of line finding can be undertaken. This is constructing a passing line. As we have noted, every track has a fastest line which is the optimum way round the course. Not unexpectedly, every rider with any sense will be on that line and thus passing will be almost impossible, hence the need for a passing line. This is an alternative route which although not necessarily the fastest overall, will enable you to get past the bloke in front. Let me give an example. A good racing line will not deal with an individual corner or straight as a separate entity but rather will blend one into another. This means that the fastest way through one corner might not actually be the racing line if it sets the rider up badly for the following section. By contrast, a passing line applies to each section on its own and is always the quickest path through any given section even if it means that the subsequent corner is then approached wrongly.

Let us consider an imaginary but realistic example. There is a fast right-hand bend followed by a rutted, bumpy straight. The straight is much smoother on the left-hand side. The racing line would require a wide approach on the outside of

*Above:* **Mervyn Anstie forces a way through on a passing line which is slower than the racing line.**

*Left:* **Picking the brains of the other riders. All the aces do it. Here Dave Watson studies form.**

the bend, probably using the berm, and then a flick on the left-hand side of the following straight. This would be used for the maximum speed. However, the passing line might require the rider to cut across the apex of the corner which would then put him on the left-hand side of the track but without the benefit of the berm. Altogether much slower. However, the advantage is that the passing line gets the rider to the exit of the corner faster than the racing line. Once there, our man can have a cup of tea and sandwiches because the lad behind cannot get past again without going on to the right-hand side of the track. This would mean that he would be slower on the following section and could not regain the lead.

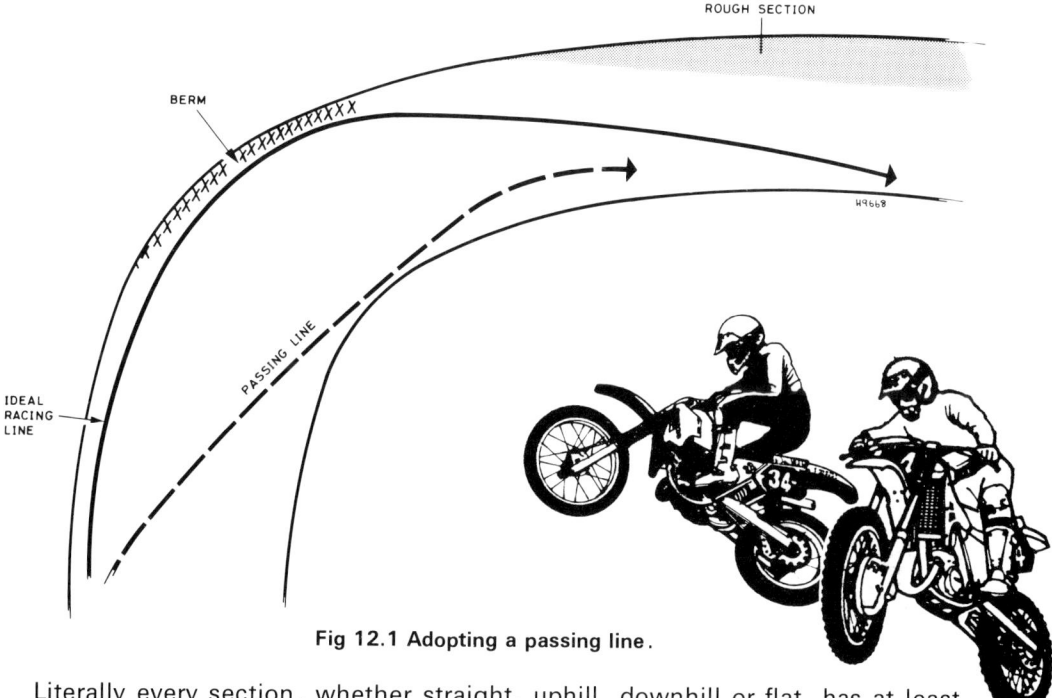

**Fig 12.1 Adopting a passing line.**

Literally every section, whether straight, uphill, downhill or flat, has at least two lines and after a few meetings you should have them firmly imprinted in your mind before a wheel ever touches the track. After the walk round, go back to the paddock and ride the track in your mind until you know every millimetre of it. Not only will you be quicker, but you will also be safer since it takes an experienced enduro rider to ride rough going quickly without knowing what lies ahead. Motocrossers need to know what is going to happen before the problem appears!

Now for the moment you have been waiting for. The chance to get out with the other bikes and show your merits. First let me say that if you feel nervous, this is neither abnormal nor anything which should cause embarrassment. Just writing about practice has made my hands go damp and my stomach tighten. If you were scared, you wouldn't be racing in the first place. What you are feeling is nervous tension and your fear is not the fear of someone who is frightened of the competition, or even of getting hurt. Rather, it is the fear of not doing well and all true competitors feel this in whatever sport they are undertaking. Blame it on the dreaded nor adrenalin again.

**Looking for the inside line.**

You will be gathered together in the collecting box whilst awaiting your turn to practice and like parking the van, there are good spots and bad ones to be in this box. The best place is at the front for two reasons. First, you are not going to get choked with the exhaust fumes from the other bikes and second, when the marshal lets you on to the track, the problem of immediately having your goggles obscured with debris as everyone burns away from the line is avoided. Since everyone else will want the same spot at the front, it will be difficult to obtain but somewhere at the side, with access to clean air — is nearly as good. When the riders are released for practice, stay where you are for a moment with your hand over your goggles to keep them clean. When the pack has disappeared, you can begin practising sensibly.

The temptation in practice is always to go racing and it takes a lot of determination to resist the competitive urge. However, it is a waste of practice to go flat out and at amateur level, there will be very little practice time available, so use it sensibly.

Check the racing lines worked out in your walk round the track and make sure that they are feasible in reality. Begin slowly, trying each bit of track separately, until the whole lap has been mastered. This will probably take two, or even three, practice sessions — and do use each one that is available to you.

When the racing line is secure in your mind, practice the passing line and if possible, try to follow a faster rider — even if only for a few hundred yards — to observe his line. Almost certainly, he will show an improvement on your line so you can copy it. Grand Prix riders are always observing each other with a view to stealing even the slightest advantage so you will be in good company!

Finally, try to get three or four laps in at your best racing speed so that you are psychologically prepared for the racing. In this last session, really attack the track and have a go at passing. It won't be easy at first but there will always be someone at your level against whom you can race. And of course, because you have applied more thought to your racing than the opposition, you are always going to get in front.

The last job to do is to study the start and the starter. We will discuss starting techniques in more detail in the next chapter but it is worth consideration of this critical skill now. Starting is the most important single act in motocross. Get a good start and it is difficult not to do well: make a bad start and you face nothing but hard work.

**Check your starter's habits before you race.**

The first task is to find yet another line. This time, the starting line. No doubt by now you will have worked out that this line will be the quickest from the start line to the first corner. If the main straight is used for starting, it will be probable that the fastest line for starting and for racing will not be the same. Instead, apply the criteria for the passing line. Above all else, get your bike into the first corner ahead of everyone else.

Obviously, this is easier said than done since everyone else will have the same idea. However, the problem can be resolved if it is thought through in stages. First, consider the track. Is it dry, wet, rock hard or offering perfect grip? On the basis of this examination will come the specific starting technique to be used. Don't worry about precisely how to get off the line — we will discuss this in great detail in the next chapter.

Next, have a good look at the starting mechanism. A lot of clubs now have metal starting gates and at Centre level, these are often less than perfect devices.

If there are practice starts, watch the gate and see if one side is quicker than the other. Elastic starting gates are usually much quicker but it is still worth checking just how the mechanism functions.

At the same time, study the starter. Does he like to keep riders on the line or is his preference for firing them away the moment they arrive? Is he calm and steady under pressure or will he panic with 35 bikes on the line? Such elements are essential to know if you are to avoid being caught unawares. For example, with a slow, methodical starter, it is not worth holding the bike in gear from the moment you arrive on the line since you may be sure that he will ensure a controlled start. By contrast, it is essential to be ready for the twitchy starter by never letting the bike out of gear and being prepared for a start almost at random.

Like confidence in one's racing line, being knowledgeable about what is going to happen on the start line gives a rider a tremendous advantage over the opposition. Frankly, I despair of riders who moan about poor starts and who have

**Dave Watson, No. 8, is on the ideal starting line and leads the British Championship race. No. 34, Mark Banks, is actually using the best racing line which, in this case, is different from the starting line, and therefore slower.**

not bothered to get off their bottoms to observe the starter at work. The starter is there to be out-thought and this requires a little effort on the part of the rider. If you won't make that effort, then be sure that some other rider will and you will be watching his tyre disappear round the first corner in every race.

I can say in all modesty that I am never beaten by a starter — unless I happen to be riding in the first race and I haven't seen him at work. Only faster riders on quicker bikes beat me into the first corner even now.

So, you have now used all your practice intelligently, you know your racing line and passing line and you have got the starts worked out. What remains to be done? Nothing, you will be pleased to know except to have a loaf around and if the track has worn badly during practice, perhaps a wander round just to clarify things in your mind. Probably you will not feel like eating much — I never do — and this is no bad thing since the amount of energy used in racing inhibits digestion and can lead to sickness. However, chocolates or sweets are easily digested and provide a quick source of energy so indulge yourself for in the next chapter, we are going racing with the grand prix stars.

# Racing!

THIS chapter has been the most fun to write and I hope it will be the most enjoyable read but before we both get carried away with our enthusiasm, I must strike a cautionary note. Some of the world's best riders helped me put this section together and just because they are the best in the world, the chances are that you will never be able to achieve their competency: otherwise, you would be one of the best riders in the world too! It follows that care **must** be exercised in trying to do some of the things I describe otherwise **you will get hurt**: it really is as simple as this. Equally, if you can't manage a double jump like Dave Thorpe after three meetings, don't be too disappointed. Remember, he is rather good!

Rather than trying to emulate the stars' riding techniques immediately, a better idea is to try to copy their attitude to racing. You can learn this from your first meeting and it will be of just as much help as mastery of riding skills.

I have been very lucky in having the help of some superb riders in researching this chapter. Dave Thorpe, Kurt Nicoll, Laurence Spence, Dave Watson, Rob Hooper and most of all, Neil Hudson, have all offered invaluable advice. Usually, I have taken the opinion of three of four riders and combined them to give a more general view of a particular strategy since each rider has his own unique view of mastering a given problem. Sometimes, one rider has the technique so right that there is no point in adding any further comment. This simply is the way to do it.

What all the stars have in common is a simple attitude to motocross. They never ride motocross, they only ever race. This difference is probably the single most important one between a club rider and a professional. Top riders attack every single section of the track as if their lives depended on it. Often they do! You will never see Thorpe or Watson having a rest on a track. They are looking for the maximum speed through every single section for every second of the race. They never cruise even if they find a particular part of the track difficult.

*Above, left:* **Professionals never ride — they only race. Here, Thorpey pursues Mark Banks with deadly determination.**

*Above, right:* **Dave Thorpe pursues Marvyn Anstie relentlessly, racing on every inch of the track.**

*Below:* **Australian star, Jeff Leisk, demonstrates the classic 'attack' position.**

This attitude is exemplefied in the riding stance. In the chapter on basic riding techniques, I described the standing position used for most riding – in serious racing, called the "attack" position. The rider is centred on the bike, legs and elbows are slightly bent and his bottom is clear of the saddle. In this position, pressure can be applied on the 'bars if necessary, the legs are ready to absorb bumps, and the rider's body weight can be transferred instantly. Ironically, although it takes good physical condition to maintain this stance, it is actually less tiring than trying to ride seated where every bump pummels the body.

In the previous chapter, I said that starting was the most important part of the race. Lead and everyone else has to catch you. Work your way from the back and the job is doubly hard. We have already discussed the importance of working out the strategy which is likely to be employed by the starter. Now, we will consider the actual starting technique itself.

**The correct position for commencing the starting sequence.**

One of the fastest starters in the world is Dave Watson and he has an unusual but effective pyschological trick to help him gate well. As the last few moments tick away before the race begins, he concentrates on the exit of the first corner and sees himself there, in the lead. It might seem strange to try to wish yourself into the lead but the ploy is very effective in that it cuts out all extraneous influences. So often at amateur level, one sees riders looking at the opposition to see how they have got off the line and then turning their heads to check whether they are in front or behind as the pack hurtles down the start straight. If you have time to concentrate on what someone else is doing, then you have no chance whatsoever of leading. It is essential that you do as Dave Watson does and mentally wish yourself into that vital first corner lead.

Before the race actually starts, an area of good traction should have been established on the start. This might be achieved by burning off the top layer of slippery grass or by removing a rock or some other obstacle. There must be nothing which could cause the bike wheel to slip out of line since the straighter the bike leaves the start line, the faster it will accelerate.

As the starter is about to release the gate, bring the engine up towards peak torque which is usually somewhere in the region of two thirds throttle. Don't blip the throttle since the fraction of a second it takes to open the throttle between each blip might just coincide with the gate falling and this will cost you a couple of places into the first corner. Rather, hold the throttle steady and be ready for instant action.

The rider's precise position on the bike will vary from start to start. Sit too far forward and there will be excessive wheelspin – all of which wastes acceleration. A shade too far to the rear and the bike will loop. Ideally, you should be towards the front of the saddle with your weight across the petrol tank, ready to slide back down the saddle to increase traction as the bike gathers speed.

At one time, getting off the line merely required the clutch to be dumped and the rider to hang on to the bike. Now it is essential to slip the clutch for a considerable distance away from the line, regardless of the bike's capacity class. The 500s in particular, pose a major difficulty.

Kurt Nicholl, who races the awesomely powerful factory KTMs in the 500 cc World Championship, sums up the problem posed by modern bikes in these words. "If I just dropped the clutch on the KTM, I wouldn't move an inch. It would just dig a big hole and we wouldn't go anywhere. I don't have the clutch fully home for at least 100 metres and on a start straight where there is a lot of traction, it will be even longer than this. You have to be completely sure that you won't waste acceleration through wheelspin before you get the clutch in."

On a 125, the clutch is slipped for a different reason. The tiny motors must be kept revving to produce their best power and if the clutch if fed in too quickly, then the engine revs will fall below the level where effective power is produced.

The easiest bikes to start are the 250s which have enough torque to get off the line quickly and easily but not so much that wheelspin is an excessive problem. With a 250, the rider also has a choice of gears for starting. In wet or slippery conditions, second might be the answer whilst first – with plenty of clutch to avoid wheelspin – might be better on a track with a lot of drive. A 125 will always be started in first gear and third will usually be the favourite for a 500.

On the two smaller capacities, gear changes will have to be made very rapidly so the left foot will need to be on the footrest whilst the right one should be in front of the footrest. Having the foot in front of the footrest encourages the rider's

Watson comes to the line and checks the starter.

The gate begins to drop and already Watson has begun feeding the clutch home in a few tenths of a second. Note the riding position.

The throttle is flat against the stop but the clutch is still being slipped. The front wheel just hovers over the ground.

Still slipping the clutch, Watson leaves the gate absolutely straight, with no wheelie.

*Above, left:* **The clutch is still being slipped as Watson makes yet another holeshot, leaving this field of British Championship stars trailing in his wake.**

*Above, right:* **Side view of the perfect start, this time with Neil Hudson. Note how straight Hudson leaves the line.**

weight to be well forward and is also safer. There is always a danger — and a very real one too — that when the bike scorches off the line, the rider's feet will drag behind and hook up in the rear tyre. Once a 5.10 x 18 Dunlop gets its teeth into your riding boot, you will be off the bike for sure — and with a good chance of a serious injury as well.

The 500s require no gear changing and so both feet can be placed in front of the footrests, which also adds a trifle more stability — no bad thing when trying to control one of these rocketships!

**The power-slide at its elegant best. Dave Thorpe's leg and boot are not used for support — only to assist balance.**

Not unnaturally, after the start straight there comes a corner so let us consider how to deal with a variety of these. First, the hard-packed or fairly smooth bend. The best way of negotiating this type of corner is still the power-slide. Using the bike's power to turn the bike is the quickest way of actually getting round the bend and also maximizes acceleration after it. Both featues are eminently desirable in racing. In the chapter on basic riding techniques, I described how to correct a power-slide by turning the 'bars into the direction of the slide. Now, we actually want to provoke the slide. The theory is still the same, but the better you become at this art, the less front wheel has to do and the more important become balance and throttle control. Kurt Nicoll is particularly fond of the power-slide and he describes the technique in these words:

"The slide starts just with the momentum of the bike as it goes into the corner. Heavy braking helps as well. As you get the bike right down the rear end will naturally want to step out. As it does, grab a good handful of throttle and the slide will start. If you've got your leg out this can help balance the bike but it slows you

down. Carla can power-slide a bike feet up all the time so it shows it can be done. Your weight should be centred on the bike and then move to the front because as the rear wheel slides, it will also drive and if you're too far back, the front end will come up and flip you off. Anyway, the front will wheelie a bit so the idea of the front wheel being used to control a slide is a bit silly really. What controls a slide is the throttle. Give it more throttle and the slide will increase. Give it less and will stop. It's as simple as that. You can then turn the bike by making the rear wheel step out further or keep nearer in line, depending on how tight you want to turn. Then, when you're past the apex of the bend, you get your body well forward and get it all on to drive out of the corner as quickly as possible. It's a really neat way of turning a corner!"

Again, I must stress that achieving what Kurt describes is a lot harder than reading about it and care must be taken before you try to emulate his technique.

An interesting variation of this technique is practised by 250 World Champion Neil Hudson — still technically one of the best riders in the world. Many corners are suitable in width to be driven round in a power-slide but are too rough for most riders to use the technique. But it can be done. Neil describes combining the method he uses for attacking undulating bumps — "whoops" in American motospeak — and power-sliding.

"To deal with whoops, you must keep the front end high enough to clear each one but not so high that time is wasted with the front-end waving in the air. The best way to do this is by working the throttle, just blipping it as you get to the top of each whoop so that the front wheel just skims it. A lot of riders seem to think that you can only do this in a straight line but it isn't so. You can blip the throttle and skim the wheel just the same if you are banked over. Best of all, you can do this and slide the bike, almost without thinking about it.

First, you must have your feet on the pegs so that you can move your weight around, because this trick is all about weight distribution and throttle control. Lift the front end just as if you were on the straight but lean into the corner with your weight just a bit to the rear of centre — but only a little bit. Now, as the rear wheel hits the lip of the whoop, give the bike a good squirt of throttle and the rear wheel will slide across the lip of the bump letting you turn sharper and with more power on. The quicker you turn, the more power you've got on, the faster you will be. You can control the slide both by the amount of throttle and also your body weight. Try to keep your body in a line with the bike, regardless of at what angle you are leaning."

Most riders learn to use berms early in their careers and proving that there is plenty of weight on the front wheel to stop it pushing out, getting round a berm quicker than the opposition often becomes a case of hitting it harder and getting the throttle open sooner. But there are methods of improving this basic approach. The first thing to be considered is that whilst berm bashing is spectacular to watch and fun to ride, it often is not as quick as it looks. There are two reasons for this.

*Facing page, top left:* **Lifting the front wheel over whoops. Note how Neil's weight is well forward and the front wheel is being raised by using the engine power.**

*Facing page, top right:* **Power-sliding across the whoops. Note how Neil slides the bike and lifts the front wheel at the same time.**

*Facing page, bottom:* **Hudson lands, applies power to lift the front wheel and shifts body weight to maintain the slide, whilst keeping the front wheel high enough to clear the next ridge.**

First, by its very nature, a berm is on the outside of a corner and therefore on the longest possible line around the bend. Second, since it is composed of earth excavated by bikes during the meeting, it will tend to be soft and will absorb a lot of power. This means that if the rider chooses to use the whole length of the berm, the first half of it in particular will slow him down tremendously since he will go into the bend with the power rolled off and will hit a wall of soft, energy absorbing earth.

*Right:* **Using the berm for turning corners rapidly. The rider is Neil Hudson.**

*Below:* **Turning without the berm by power-sliding round it – often a quicker method of negotiating the bend.**

This can be to his advantage because it enables very late braking simply by slamming into the wall of the berm – provided it is firm enough – and then letting the bike slow down by the impact. But there is a better way of using the braking power of the berm without spending time in the useless front portion.

1984 World Champion Andre Malherbe's technique on berms which are really solid is stay well away from the front part of the berm and instead, slide the bike across the apex of the corner feet up, with both wheels virtually locked. Just at the point where it seems inevitable that bike, rider and all must hit the ground, Malherbe cannons into the centre of the berm and still with his feet firmly on the pegs, and with his handlebars almost scraping the ground, gives his Honda a big handful of throttle and accelerates away. Thus, he uses the berm to permit acute angles of lean and early application of maximum power but does not waste time with the first, energy absorbing part of the berm.

Throughout the book, there are warnings about trying to ride beyond yourself but when I discussed Malherbe's "berm" style with Kurt Nicoll it was he who expressed a note of caution. "What you say is absolutely right. Malherbe can go round berms, feet up, just like you say. And it's the quickest, too. But you should also say that only Malherbe can do it. Not Thorpey, Jobe, Carla, me or anyone else can do the same thing safely and reliably so really there's no chance for an amateur rider.

The problem is that when Andre hits the berm feet up, the bike has effectively crashed. Really he just crashes the bike in the berm. After the crash, when he ought to be on the floor counting the broken bones, he un-crashes and squirts away. The **only**, and I mean **only**, way you can do this trick is by having a sense of timing which makes half nothing seem forever. And then you've got to get the power on really hard.

I know how to do the trick but if I tried it, I would crash every other time. The rest of us get round nearly as quick by sliding across the corners and then sitting down as we hit the berm so that we can use the inside leg for balance and to support the bike if our timing is that fraction out. With lot's of practice, a good non-professional can master this technique – but not Malherbe's. Just enjoy watching him do instead. It's more fun – and safer."

A variation on this theme is used by Dave Watson using what he calls "a

**Andy Nicholls demonstrates the "handbrake" turn.**

handbrake turn" – after the way rally car drivers lock the back wheels of their cars with the handbrake in order to flick them through tight corners. Instead of using the berm, Dave cuts in tight across the inside of the corner and lays the bike hard down. At such an acute angle of lean, the bike would simply fall over without a berm to stop it. In particular, the front end would plough away as the rider tried to turn too quickly. The solution is to jab hard at the rear brake just before the apex of the bend. Locking the rear wheel, along with the turn being made, will send the back of the bike into a slide, turning the bike very quickly.

At the same time as the rear wheel is locked, the clutch is withdrawn so that the engine doesn't stall and also to enable the clutch to be slipped on the exit to the corner. Because the bike is going too slow to maintain stability, it is essential to get the power on as quickly as possible once past the apex of the bend in order that momentum straightens it up at the same time as giving maximum acceleration.

Dave Watson squaring off a berm by sliding the bike through the apex. Note the line of the corner is almost left to right across the photograph and Watson has cut across it at virtually 90°. Note also his use of the clutch to get the motor instantly into the power band.

At its best, the whole manoeuvre should be carried out feet up so that no time is lost going from a standing to sitting position and back again and also to give the rider the maximum opportunity to maintain balance. Perhaps now the importance of total mastery of braking, as we discussed in the chapter on basic riding techniques, becomes fully apparent.

Whilst we are looking at corners it seems an appropriate moment to discuss braking and acceleration into and out of bends. Perhaps the most critical element of these skills as practised by the professionals is that they do both of them actively. Neil Hudson makes this point: "Too many ordinary riders sort of coast into the corner and then let the bike drift round at its own speed before they even open the throttle. That's just no good. You've got to go into the corner having used every last bit of the bike's braking ability and then you really open the throttle. In motocross, if you're not braking, you should be accelerating – there's no time for anything in between."

There are several mistakes which amateur riders make regarding stopping and the most common of these is to brake too early. If you brake and then have to open the throttle to actually get to the corner, then you are braking too early; there's just no excuse. Immediately you are off the brakes, you should be on the throttle to power round the corner but not to actually let you reach the bend.

The rider's weight should be towards the rear of the bike but not hanging over the rear mudguard. The reason for the weight transfer is that as the front brake is applied hard, the forks will dip and the rear end will rise. At this point, the rear suspension is effectively too stiff for the job it is trying to do since there is so little load on it. Often, the rear end will kick up into the air. Try riding like this on severe bumps into a bend and the rear end will kick around leading to what is known as a "tank-slapper". This crowd-pleasing activity is usually followed by a short trip over the 'bars and then a test of how quick the rider can crawl to the side of the track before he is pounded to pieces by the rest of the entry following him.

The solution, strangely, it to put a little power on as you go into the corner. The power loads the suspension and makes it work more effectively whilst at the same time reducing the diving of the front forks, giving them a chance to work too.

The key to success is not to slam on the brakes at the last second and then fight the resultant tank-slapper. Rather, brake hard but smoothly using the brakes and throttle and your body weight to decelerate the bike as quickly as possible but without ever losing control of it. Braking is a critical skill and it is worth studying a really smooth rider like Neil or Dave Thorpe to see how quickly they stop but without ever resorting to brute strength to slow their bikes.

*Below, left:* **The back-end starts to kick as Hudson brakes hard – even though his weight is well to the rear.**

*Below, right:* **Neil applies some power to bring it down whilst still braking hard.**

Neil also stresses smoothness when it comes to applying power on the exit to corners. Occasionally, such as when he hits a big, loose berm, there is an opportunity for snapping open the throttle and hanging on but usually, the bike goes quicker if the power is applied smoothly and with the rider in control. No more so is this more apparent than when dealing with those square edged holes which are a feature of the exits of many motocross courses today. These are caused by the bikes themselves forming bumps which become magnified as successive rear wheels dig more and more earth out of the valleys.

If these bumps are hit badly, then all sorts of problems will result — the worst ones resulting yet again in short duration flying lessons. The reason that they can cause so much difficulty is due to the suspension forced to work in a manner not suited to it.

The rider comes out of the corner with the power on, the front forks hit the top of the bump and they compress. As the crest is reached, the front wheel plops into the next valley and the forks extend whilst the rear wheel kicks up because it has too little load on it so the bike progresses, rocking-horse fashion, until a crash occurs.

The solution is to clear the crest of the bump without the front wheel touching. As the front wheel approaches the crest, slip the clutch just a little and this will give a burst of power sufficient to wheelie over the bump, leaving the forks completely unloaded to deal with the subsequent landing in the next valley and equally important, keeping the rear suspension working effectively, because the power will not only aid acceleration but will also pull it down. Again, the answer to the problem is the smooth, thoughtful application of power rather than just relying on brute force and courage.

*Below:* **Braking on hills must be done wherever there is an opportunity. Here, Neil jumps the first part of the hill and prepares to brake . . .**

*Facing page:* **. . . and then brakes on the relatively smooth part of the hill which follows . . .**

**. . . before opening the throttle and accelerating for the next downhill jump.**

The same techniques can be used for dealing with bumps on the straight and most riders these days, aided by bikes which flatter their riding ability, seem to be able to go quickly in a straight line even when the track is rough. The problem comes when the straight line is not flat but goes uphill or downhill.

Neil's attitude towards descents and ascents is straightforward. "They're just like any other part of the track but turned on their side. The biggest mistake you can make is thinking that a downhill corner is different than a flat corner. It isn't. It's just pointed a different way!"

Again, the key to riding downhills successfully is throttle control and body positioning. All downhills should be ridden with the rider's weight slightly to the rear of the centre of balance but as always, not so far back that the arms become straight and are unable to absorb shocks properly. Because of the angle of the descent, the front forks will be unnaturally loaded and as we have already discussed, the way to get them and the rear suspension to work properly is to get some power on — even if it is only a little bit. Neil descends hills by changing up through the gears, just as if he were on a flat straight, and this makes the bike's suspension perform as well as possible. Bumps which require wheelieing over can be dealt with in the normal fashion just as if the track were flat. But what about jumps? These too can be done just as well as on the flat, keeping to same rules about rear wheel landings if possible.

At one time, it used to be suggested to riders that when they attempted a downhill jump, they needed to haul back on the bars and transfer their body dramatically to the rear of the bike to prevent the front wheel landing first on a downhill slope and pitching the rider over the bars. This technique was essential on very heavy, cumbersome bikes which were slow to react to rider input but today, there is no need for such dramatic antics. On a downhill jump, merely retaining the normal "attack" position will ensure that the bike drops away from you and naturally assumes the ideal rear wheel landing posture. However, it should be noted that it is vital to get some power on instantly on landing to prevent the front end making an excessively heavy return to earth.

The same rules apply to corners and braking on hills as they do for the flat bits of the track — only more so! Because the front forks will be loaded on a downhill descent, it is essential to get any braking necessary to negotiate a bend well finished before tackling the obstacle. Clearly, it is foolish to expect the forks to deal with the triple stresses of downhill loading, braking and being slammed into a corner. So, get your braking finished before the corner and then with intelligent use of the throttle, the load can be eased on the front forks as the corner is negotiated. As we have already established, this will give the rear suspension the chance to work properly as well.

Kurt Nicoll added to Neil's assessment by saying that it is possible to carry out any manoeuvre on a downhill bend that you can on a flat corner. The key thing is that you must be accelerating through the obstacle at the time. This means that downhill braking might have to be done at places which are not the optimum for racing braking but allow safe slowing down. You can then accelerate towards the corner, bump or drop with power-on. This means finding the smoothest bit on the hill, braking on it to a speed which will enable you to manage the rest of the descent, and then getting the power on to make the suspension work.

Climbs are not so pyschologically daunting. After all, if the throttle is shut the bike will stop and that will be an end to your ascent, but once again, racing these parts of the track, as distinct from riding on them, is another matter. Inevitably, we come back to throttle control and body position once again but this time, more than at any other, you must get out of the saddle and get the body weight well forward. Perhaps the hardest thing to do on an uphill is to jump and at the risk of sounding repetitive, uphill jumping is just like any other form except that the rider must get his weight well to front of the bike and he must land with the throttle shut — at least for the first few milli-seconds after landing — since this is essential to bring the front wheel to earth and also to avoid a "mega-wheelie" which would cause the bike to flip.

Probably the single thing the stars do so much better than us ordinary mortals is to jump a bike. Seeing Kurt Nicoll hurtle through air for what seems like hours always leaves me in wonder at how such feats can be achieved. Riding skill has a lot to do with it but superb physical fitness and also an economy size dose of sheer courage also help considerably. Given these three attributes, it is possible to do quite remarkable things with a bike whilst it is in the air. First, sorting out the problems.

As we have said many times, if you begin to jump with the power on, then the bike will sail through the air and land on the rear wheel. Conversely, take-off with the power off and it will describe a parabola and land front wheel first, usually — but not always — leading to a crash. So what happens if you get in a tangle and the bike is heading for a front wheel landing? The first thing to do it not to panic. Modern front forks are going to get you out of trouble 95 times out of 100. We are only considering the last 5% now. The most obvious thing to do — and the most sensible — is to pull back on the 'bars to lift the front end of the bike. At the same time, push the bike away from you with your feet. Remember, the bike is effectively pivoting around the soles of your feet so it is possible to move the mass quite dramatically. Lastly, open up the throttle and the mass of the spinning rear wheel will actually pull down the rear end to a quite dramatic degree. Clearly, all these tactics require considerable practice and again, I should warn that these are techniques used by experienced professional riders and are not necessarily practical, or even possible, by amateur competitors.

If the take-off has been spoilt by poor body positioning with the rider too far to the rear, the bike will tend to adopt an excessively steep posture in the air. The danger now is that when the landing occurs, the bike will loop. The solution this time is first to try to get some body weight well forward to bring down the front end and then, if this fails, land with the throttle closed and immediately apply some rear brake. Unfortunately this trick will tend to bring the front end crashing down to earth so immediately the danger of looping is over, give the bike a burst of throttle to lift it again. Once more, a technique which requires some considerable skill and practice.

The very best riders can turn the bike in mid-air with some accuracy. This is useful both for impressing would-be sponsors and also for racing for if a rider can turn his bike in mid-air before he lands, he can often achieve a better racing line through the next corner. I take this section almost entirely from Kurt Nicoll since I freely admit that I can scarcely imagine how to achieve what he describes.

"First of all, you've got to know what you want to do before you're in the air. That's really very, very important. You've not the time to think about it when you're actually flying. When you're in the air, you push on the inside of the bike and that will turn it the way you want to land. You can then move your body inwards to straighten it up or to lay the bike over even more. When you land, the power should already be on hard and the bike will straighten up almost on its own and off you go again. Nothing to it really!"

Still the most spectacular feat in riding for both the rider and spectator, is the double jump. All the aces who helped with this section are masters of the double jump but none more so than Dave Thorpe.

**Paul Hunt getting "radical" with his flying.**

**Russ Vernon gives a superb demonstration of turning the bike in flight.**

"The first thing you need to do a double is a lot of bottle. Then you need a fair bit of riding skill as well. You approach the bottom of the first part of the double standing and with your weight slightly to the rear and in as high a gear as possible. You need a lot of speed to do this and the engine has got to be pulling well. At the bottom of the start of the double, try to get the bike flat out in whatever gear you are using. You should have moved a bit closer towards the centre of the bike and be ready for the impact as you hit the bottom of the double hard.

You fly up the first slope in a flash and as you reach the top, close the throttle a little and the bike will go through the air for a front wheel landing. Keep the throttle closed in the air pushing the bike through your legs and down. The bike will now be nicely set up for a front wheel landing on the downward slope of the second part of the double. As the bike lands, the power should be on to take the load off the front forks — and away you go!"

Before doing this, try to reach at least expert status, for whilst all that Dave describes is quite straightforward for a World Champion, it is very different for us lesser mortals.

I shall finish this chapter by mentioning a few of the things you ought to know but perhaps other books don't tell you. These techniques too, are straight from mouths of professional racers and they reflect the mental and physical toughness necessary to do well at professional levels.

First passing. Dave Watson says, "There's nothing magic about passing someone, it's just a matter of wanting to get by. The mistake most amateur riders

Dave Thorpe sets his Grand Prix Honda up for the landing after a big double jump. Note the critical importance of landing front wheel first.

make is that they start following the man in front instead of racing him. They become hypnotised by his back wheel and when they do this, they'll never get past. I like to go for a quick, clean pass using skill rather than barging my way through."

David's attitude is reflected by the world's top two riders Andre Malherbe and Dave Thorpe. Both of these riders race at 110% giving not an inch and yet one rarely sees them come into physical contact with each other. This is motocross at its best.

Unfortunately, some riders rely more on brute force than skill and you should be aware of what happens when racing against a rider of this type. The rule of thumb is that if your back wheel is hit by another rider's front, then he will come off worse. In fact, hitting any part of another bike with your front wheel is likely to bring you off the loser. However, by laying a rear wheel alongside another bike and tweaking the throttle, the rear end will step out — often into the front wheel —

and the results are usually disastrous for the recipient. A variation on this move is the "rut block". One rider is being closely followed by another in a rut. The leading rider whips in his clutch and jabs the front brake causing the follower to hit his back wheel and stall, thus removing any chances of overtaking on the next open section of the course. Again, not really sporting but nevertheless still done in motocross.

I don't advocate these tactics for a moment nor do any of the riders who have helped with this section but it is as well to be aware of them so that you can take avoiding action if you do come across an unsporting rider.

However, there are times when physical presence can be useful. For example, it is perfectly legitimate to keep poking your front wheel into the line of sight of the rider in front – the expression is "showing him your wheel" – even if you can't pass. Unless your opponent is particularly cool and not given to panic, this pressure will fluster him into making a mistake which will allow you to pass. An

**The ultimate double jump! Georges Jobe at Hawkstone. You need a lot of courage as well as skill and physical fitness for this exercise.**

equally good variation on this strategy is to show your wheel on one side until the opposition becomes sure that this is where you will pass and then make a quick dive for the blind side.

Having a real good shout at the same time is also perfectly legitimate. In fact, when you get good enough to lap riders, it is often a good idea to give a shout to get them out of your way for their safety as well as your speed.

One cautionary note should be added about "showing a wheel". I have already stressed that the front wheel is the most vulnerable part of the bike so be careful about exposing it at any point where your opponent could simply cut across you. If he clips the front wheel with something solid – like the engine rail or his rear wheel, then you will be off. The idea is to continuously make him aware of your presence without getting close enough to suffer physical attack.

**The block pass exemplified. Here, Kurt Nicoll has "done the job" on Brett Steele.**

A common mistake amateur riders make is to be too worried about the performance of the opposition and not enough about their own. This is manifested in continuously looking round to see how the man behind is faring. It is better to choose one spot on the course – a 180° hairpin bend is ideal – to check on the progress of the people behind you and for the rest of the lap, concentrate on your riding. If you are in imminent danger of being passed you will be all too well aware of the problem. If not, a single check will do.

Better still is to have a signaller but this is luxury which might not come for some time. Only someone who really loves the rider will stand next to the track getting covered in clag whilst the rider dices for 27th place in the non-winner's consolation race. However, assuming that you are lucky enough to be cared for that much there are two things which are vital to successful signalling. The first is to ensure that you can see the message. This means having your signaller choose a spot where you are approaching him on a straight course and preferably slowing down. It is less than useless having your pit-board on the outside of a fast sweeper when you are going away from it. Equally bad is a section of very rough or narrow track which demands all your attention. Rather, pick a site where you have time to find your signaller, spot the message, and read it without hazarding yourself or other riders. This might sound like an impossible set of criteria but it is surprising how soon you will develop the knack.

A big help in effective signalling is to include the minimum message on the pit-board; you don't need a great long story merely what information you feel is essential. This varies from rider to rider but I only ever asked for my place and whether I was gaining on the rider in front. A waved finger of warning advised me if I was being caught rapidly. It is nice to know when the last two laps are taking place so that you can either make that last desperate effort to get into the trophies or know that suffering has only got to last another five minutes and you can enjoy a hero's welcome back in the paddock. After all, 27th is a good result if your previous best was 28th!

**Keith Thorpe provides the essential minimum of information for Dave.**

# Sponsorship

I suppose every racer's dream is of sponsorship. The factory mechanic, palatial motor home and fabulous wages must represent heaven on earth to most riders and there are very few of us who would not swop places with Andre Malherbe or Dave Thorpe. Yet, as with many things in life, the idea is often more attractive than the reality. Not that the life-style of the world's top riders is anything to be sneered at. The very best do very well indeed and they have all the necessary home comforts which accompany international success. But these super-stars most certainly do not get paid for doing nothing. They are totally devoted to their business — for them motocross is not a sport in any sense of the word — and whilst the rewards are high, the price of failure is equally clear. It is true that a few — a very, very few — riders do make a lot of money from motocross but most professional riders do no better than if they were working in a factory — with the notable exception that there is much more job satisfaction!

I am stressing the two sides to sponsorship simply because it may be that for you, the problems associated with sponsorship at any level outweigh the advantages. In fact, the first step on the road to sponsorship is to decide whether you actually do want to pay the personal price for the help you receive. If you do, then read on. If not, then this is an equally sensible decision and you should be given every credit for making it. Having a sponsor may sound impressive, but in reality, it can be so much trouble that your racing is spoilt. If you are earning $600,000 a year, then it is reasonable to expect a lot of aggravation. Is the same true if motocross is your hobby? I cannot answer for you but do think about both sides of the argument. Remember, he who pays the piper calls the tune — even if the piper doesn't like the melody!

Let's begin by looking at why a rider is sponsored. I have seen both sides of the sponsorship fence and the view is very different depending on whether you are the recipient or the provider of sponsorship. I have enjoyed being sponsored by many companies over the years and I am still helped by Eddie Crooks Motorcycles, at Barrow-in-Furness. As a rider, I always wanted sponsorship to reduce my vast expenditure and enable me to do as well as possible in my racing. However, my main involvement with motocross is now as Rooster Reeds' Racing Co-Ordinator. This position involves me being largely responsible for spending thousands of pounds of Rooster Reeds' money and I am trusted to use my racing budget intelligently. What does "intelligently" mean in this context? A very simple question which can be answered in one word: sales. The money I spend on racing is for one thing and one thing alone, that is to promote sales. If my efforts don't help sales then there is no reason at all for Rooster to employ me — and I feel sure that they wouldn't! So lesson number one is that companies sponsor riders not to win races, nor get mentions in the motorcycling media, but first, last and middle to generate sales.

This basic point is misunderstood by so many riders that one could assume that it was a state secret. Perhaps it is, but nevertheless it is the single most important factor — one could say the only factor — in getting and keeping sponsorship.

At this stage, let us digress a little to say that there is another form of sponsorship other than the strictly commercial kind given by Kawasaki, Clover or Arai helmets. Sponsorship which comes as a gift is the best kind of all and is worth far more than commercial help of twice the value. This philanthropic help might come from parents, or girl-friends or even a local company with an interest in racing. I was once sponsored by a firm of jewellers because the managing director's son happened to be interested in bikes at the time. It was really a perfect arrangement. They gave me a few hundred pounds and I put two stickers on the bike and entertained the family at one meeting. Other than that, no-one took any notice of what I did or what results I obtained — a situation which was improved even further when the son discovered that girls were somewhat different

**The author's Crooks-Suzuki, ready to race. All the sponsor's stickers are in their correct places and the bike is neat and tidy to create a good impression.**

from boys and lost his interest in bikes altogether.

This kind of sponsor is beyond value since because they are not commercial in intent, they will be far more enthusiastic about your success and infinitely more forgiving of your failings than a company which is seeking return on its investment. If you are lucky enough to find such a sponsor, for goodness sake hang on to him like grim death. Should this mean kissing Uncle Boris's Great Dane, or playing coochy-coo with your sister's repulsive first-born son, then do it. Philanthropic sponsors are worth their weight in gold and often – usually – of greater worth than any commercial help much below a full factory contract.

However, such benefactors are rare so let's have a look at the more common road towards easing the financial burden of racing. We have already established that commercial sponsorship means generating sales and whilst this is possible at a surprisingly early stage in a rider's career, it is clearly not going to happen until he has some credibility. This means that what you have to say must influence someone. Now, if you have just finished a tactical 31st in the Junior "B" race, then clearly, you aren't going to have a lot of influence over anybody – except perhaps the poor soul who finished 32nd. This being the case, trying for sponsorship is rather optimistic. A more callous writer than me would say a total waste of time – but I have always lived in optimism so I will not say "total", only 99.99% useless.

However, by the time you have worked your way up to expert status – in the AMCA or ACU – it is reasonable to start thinking about some help. But what makes you different from all the other expert riders in your club and centre – and there are plenty of them? Well, you must try to develop credibility and this means making your opinions influence other riders.

There are a number of ways you can do this. An obvious one is by winning races

**Three members of the KTM factory team demonstrate how professionals promote their sponsors. First, Kurt Nicoll carefully kneels in the mud so the crowd can see his KTM logo ...**

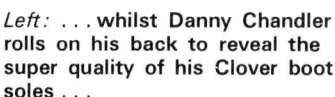

*Left:* . . . whilst Danny Chandler rolls on his back to reveal the super quality of his Clover boot soles . . .

*Below:* . . . and Jack Van Velthoven stops in mid-Grand Prix to allow a member of the public to feel the quality of his M. Robert jeans.

and many riders think that this is only, or even most important gambit. In fact, winning is only a small part of the package. For example, if you win a race and your bike hasn't been washed for a month then there is little use in trying to convince someone that Rock Oil's maintenance spray is the greatest thing since knobbly tyres. Your bike, your clothing and your attitude are all vehicles for promoting yourself.

Let's take an example. You have just finished second in a race and a junior comes across and asks you about the Dunlop tyres you have been using. What do you do? The worst possible thing is to collapse in a heap and take no notice of his enquiries. Perhaps there is one worse — if you told him to "Naff off!" and stop annoying you. Hopefully, he would get his mate to torpedo you in the next race and break your leg. Such arrogance would be justly rewarded.

However, what if you told him how pleased you were with the tyre and what good value it was and then finished by telling him of the local dealer who sold it to you. With a bit of luck, the lad would trot into the dealer next Saturday and might quote your recommendation as he too, bought the tyre. Perhaps this situation is somewhat idealistic but the general principle does work — provided the rider is sufficiently intelligent to make it work.

In practice, most riders tend to be short-sighted in the extreme and really fail to gain any sponsorship before they have even started. They argue their case like this. "Until, I am sponsored, I am not doing anything for anybody. If they want my help, they've got to pay me for it. The dealer thinks, "That's a real lazy sproat. He never does anything for anybody. There's no point in sponsoring him. He's too idle." Unfortunately for the rider, the dealer is always right since he would be giving to the rider — not the other way about.

You will notice that I have begun the discussion about sponsorship with the dealer. This is for the very important reason that most initial sponsorship will come from a dealer. At Rooster Reeds, all our first level sponsorship comes through dealers and we gradually move the very best dealer-sponsored riders on to direct factory contracts so this help is not only important in its own right but is also a vital first foot on the rung of the ladder.

Clearly, the better terms you are on with your local shop then the more likely you are to receive some help. If you flit around from one dealer to another for the sake of a few extra pounds discount, then this is not going to help you gain assistance from any given trade source. Conversely, if you buy regularly from one shop, then you can build up the sort of relationship which encourages the first little bits of help.

You can encourage this initial move by acting responsibly and sensibly in the shop. Look for ways of showing that you have product knowledge and that you are willing to use that knowledge to the dealer's advantage. For example, a lad comes in for a pair of boots and is unsure what to buy, can you offer him some advice? This does not mean hitting him with high pressure sales techniques but rather offering genuine, practical advice which will result in a sale for the dealer. Which make of boot doesn't really matter, provided that the customer leaves the shop with something — and that you have been instrumental in promoting that sale.

Now through the dealer's eyes, this is good news. He sees a rider who will actually work for the good of the business and he will be very impressed, if only because of the rarity of the situation. His response could well be to offer you a new pair of boots at a discount price. This is the second major hurdle to cross. At this stage, very many riders will say, "Oh, I've only had £10 worth of help, so I'm only going to do £10 worth of work for it." This is the road to disaster.

**ALL** initial sponsorship is more trouble than its value. Now you begin to see why I questioned the value of sponsorship at all. For the little bit of discount you have received, you have now not only to promote the dealer's boots but also his tyres, chains, jeans, oil and bikes — all of which have produced nothing for you at the start.

But let's look at it through the dealer's eyes again. What does he see? For a very modest outlay — he has probably only sacrificed his profit on the boots so he has actually not spent anything at all — he has gained a zealous salesman who is actually helping with sales. What an encouragement to help even further. So, when the Clover boot representative calls round the dealer mentions you and your efforts and maybe, just maybe, a free pair of boots arrives.

By this time, you will be gaining a reputation as a rider worth sponsoring. All sponsors talk to each other and largely, riders will be desirable to them all or to none. The classic example is Dave Thorpe. Polite, articulate, superbly turned out, patient with fans and a Grand Prix winner. Really, there is not a sponsor who would not go out on a limb to find the last penny to secure Dave's services. Yet, there are other Grand Prix riders who always seem to struggle getting good sponsors. Ask yourself why.

Now, if you add some race successes to this picture of a hard working, knowledgeable and commercially aware rider, there becomes every reason to begin some real investment in him.

This is primarily the reason why some AMCA riders do so very well. Whilst they are nowhere as fast as the best ACU International runners, they are far more commercially aware and make the best use of the influence they have within their sport and as a result, they do very well. The top AMCA experts are getting free bikes, spares, clothing, oil and accessories and that sort of package is worth a lot of money.

This brings us once again to the central issue of sponsorship. Is it really worth the effort? The picture I have painted of the ideal rider to sponsor is one which not only shows him as a dedicated rider, with top-class machine preparation, but also the sort of lad who is willing to work hard at promotion during his Sunday's sport. It may well be that for you, this ruins the best day of the week and if it does, I would not blame you for a moment for adopting this point of view. There is a lot to be said for turning up at a race, having a gossip with your friends, riding and then going home. I rode for several years like this.

On the other hand, most riders derive pleasure from receiving some recognition for their efforts. Grand Prix riders are always sulking about being pestered by fans but let no-one ask them for an autograph at a meeting and they immediately start worrying that they have lost their star appeal. Yes, having one's value appreciated is very nice too!

The financial benefits are also very welcome. I have spent tens of thousands of pounds of my own money racing and it doesn't bear thinking about what the cost would have been without the many sponsors who have helped me.

However, the more money involved in a contract, then the more the sponsor will expect in return. A Grand Prix contract will not only specify how the rider is to be paid for a given race place but exactly what clothes he will wear during the race and in the paddock, where each badge will be placed on his shirt and even the number and size of the stickers on his bike and van. At this level, there is very little room for personal friendship and whilst a team manager may, or may not, like a rider personally, his prime concern will be whether that rider can execute his contract fully and effectively.

Although I now negotiate such contracts, I never received them personally and so I was in the pleasant position of being friends with all my sponsors. In fact, this is probably the greatest benefit from being sponsored: you can collect some super friends and get paid for the privilege as well.

To conclude, if you go for sponsorship, go for it properly and try to set yourself up as the sort of rider I have described in this chapter. Work hard at your job and you can be well re-paid not only financially but in terms of status and the friends you will make.

If sponsorship doesn't appeal to you, then this is equally acceptable and just as sensible. In this case, don't look for that which you don't want. It will only cause you, and your sponsor, needless heartache.

# A week
# in the life of a champion

THROUGHOUT this book, I have tried to stress that the most important thing in motocross is not winning but having fun. If the bike is running well, and the track good, beating your best mate for tenth place can provide enough satisfaction to last the week and give life a very rosy glow. Not everyone can be a winner, and even fewer of us can ever achieve any national recognition, so there is little use in making the acquisition of fame or success the main reason for racing. Riding a motocross bike is some of the best fun on earth and racing it even more so. If success comes as well, then this is really the icing on the cake.

If you are good, then winning becomes important. The better the rider you are, the more success becomes an essential part of racing and the harder it is to achieve since inevitably, the competition is composed entirely of riders with the same idea. At the very highest level, every rider is a star in his own right and to win a Grand Prix requires a very special sort of rider. He will be a more than superb athlete and complete master of the motorcycle, more even than a fine race technician. Above all else, he will have a single-minded determination which is almost frightening in its intensity.

Talk to any world class rider and their desire to succeed throbs out like a beacon and leaves the determination we ordinary mortals demonstrate as scarcely more than a passing whim.

Even amongst this special breed, one young rider is making a name for himself. That rider is Dave Thorpe, a rider utterly determined to be the world's best motocross rider and one who is pursuing this aim with ruthless efficiency. Yet taken away from the bike, Dave is modest to the point of shyness and gentle in thought and word.

This chapter tells the story of a week in the life of Dave Thorpe. If you aspire to the very top, then you could do much worse than model yourself on David. Note

Dave Thorpe.

his near-obsession with looking after the needs of Honda and his supplementary sponsors. Look at his determination in training and practice. Finally, remember that this interview was conducted two weeks after Dave had won the British Grand Prix in front of fifteen thousand adoring fans. His reaction: " I'm nothing special. The fact that I can ride a bike a bit better than most doesn't make me Superman. I'm just lucky I'm good at doing something I also enjoy. You know, I'm only a star on Sunday and that doesn't make me very important does it?" A philosophy as sound as this is worth remembering after you have won your first race. Dave takes up the story!

"Monday is rest day. It varies tremendously, depending on what happened on the Sunday. After Hawkstone, (Dave's first G.P. win), it was great. I felt really good, not only because I won the race, but because I had done so much for Honda and for the fans. It was the second best day of my life. The best day was the birth of my son. That was more important than winning any race.

Winning an important race or championship is a really good feeling but it doesn't last too long. A professional rider is only as good as his last race so by the end of Monday, I've got to start looking to the next race. Perhaps I'll feel better for longer when I win the World Championship.

I'm glad that I don't stay too excited for long because the same applies to a bad day. I remember Carlsbad this year, (in 1984, Dave had a disastrous day at the American Grand Prix), and how low I felt after this one race. You know, it was terrible seeing all the training and effort disappear in one afternoon. I just couldn't believe it. Then I thought, the result only lasts until the next race and as soon as I started back at training, my mind was on the next race. Looking back all the time is no good for a professional racer.

I don't do any training at all on Monday but instead I try to take it really easy. If

**Dave, Sharon and Lewis.**

Sharon (Dave's wife), has got some music on, I'll listen to this or maybe I'll watch some television or go shopping. Remember, I'm a husband and dad as well as a motocross rider.

Monday is washday too. Sharon washes all my race shirts herself. I use about fifteen at a meeting and I probably have the same number of spares. It is important for my sponsors that I look really smart on the track so every time I go out, I wear clean shirt and jeans. During a season, I'll use about thirty pairs of jeans and probably fifteen pairs of boots and the same number of helmets. This might seem like a lot of gear but just think what the club riders would think of me if I started a Grand Prix wearing tatty gear. That wouldn't be much good to my sponsors.

I clean and my boots and helmets and the jeans go to the laundry. Thirty pairs of jeans plus Lewis's nappies would be a bit much even for a wife as keen as Sharon! In the evening, we watch TV. I'm not a great television fan and I'm easily pleased so I'll watch what Sharon enjoys. She's got a quick temper and so it's safer for me this way! About nine o'clock, we're getting ready for bed. I'm starting to think about training tomorrow and Sharon is wondering how many times Lewis will get us up in the night.

Tuesday, work starts. I should make it clear that the week I'm describing is a summer week. I want to make this point because in winter, I do the real work in the gym. In summer, it's important that you don't do too much work and take the fine edge of your physical performance. You need your best effort for the track and it would be really stupid to kill yourself in the gym. There's nobody to race against there and no prize money either. So, in summer, I'm just keeping up the condition I've built during the winter. Racing keeps my fit anyway.

I don't follow a set diet although we're looking at this for next year. I start off the day with three *Shredded Wheat* and some orange juice, probably followed by toast and coffee. I need the energy for later on.

By eight o'clock I'm down at Bracknell Sports Centre. It's only a ten minute drive from home and the facilities are really good. My first job is to run for an hour and I hate EVERY minute of it. Before I broke my leg, I used to like running and I always found it easy at school but I was so long laid up that I really dislike it now. That's all the more reason for doing it. It's self-discipline which is as important as the actual running. I've got a good course laid out which goes from the Sports Centre and into the woods. There's a variety of terrain with some climbs which are a good challenge when you're getting tired.

**Being a World Champion is all about effort.**

I also practise running the best line round each corner. This might seem funny at 6mph, but I pretend I'm on a bike and it's a race track. I look for little tiny changes in the track. You know, like a puddle or a stick fallen across the path. Then I work really hard thinking about how to deal with the problem — even though it's nothing. There is a reason for this — honest! When I started to go really quick in G.P.s I found that I was losing concentration during a race. There's a lot of mental effort involved in racing at this level and I think working so hard physically plus the mental effort involved was making me lose concentration — and you can't afford this even for a second when you've got Georges Jobes or Andre on your tail. So, as I run, I work my body and brain and it's all the more valuable because I don't like doing it.

When I've finished the run, I know that things are going to get better throughout the day. I work at the weights in the gym, exercising each group of muscles but all the time keeping plenty in reserve for the race on Sunday. As I said, in summer it's just a case of keeping in trim.

About 12 o'clock, I ring Sharon and ask if she feels like lunch. Sometimes we'll have a meal at home or I might go to this little bakery near the sports centre where they sell filled rolls. They're really good, made from wholewheat bread, and I can soon shift a pile of those. After I've got the rolls, I dash home in the Porsche. It's black and goes really well. It was a present to myself last year and I enjoy driving it a lot. I must be the fastest breadman in the south!

**One of the benefits of being a World Champion.**

The afternoon changes from week to week. Usually I go practising, or I might be dad again to Lewis, but usually practising is the most important. Most of the time, I go to Kingsclere, which is the nearest decent track to us. I always have one works bike here to use, even if Keith ( Dave's father and full time mechanic) is in Belgium doing the other two. It's identical to my race bikes so I can practise with confidence.

Practising is the time when I don't mind falling off. There's no use practising if you don't try hard and in fact, I go harder practising than when racing. This is the time when I'm finding my limits – the real edge of my ability. When I race I hardly ever take chances because I know just how far I can go without overdoing it. The other thing which is important is to ride for the same amount of time as you will be racing. In my case, I always go out for 50 minutes. That's just a little longer than a Grand Prix. This gives me stamina to race just as hard as I practise.

Wednesday usually starts off like Tuesday except that sometimes, I won't have time to go training because of business commitments. However, I do try to fit some training in during the day. I work for Dave Thorpe Racing Ltd. The truth is, I'm the company's only rider but at my level, you've got to run yourself professionally. I'm lucky having a job I like doing and I want to do it well. If I can also make some money, then things will be really good. What I don't want to do is make money and then waste it. I've seen that happen to a lot of riders and I don't want it to happen to me.

At present, Honda are the best company in the world to work for. They are so professional and dedicated to winning the World Championships that any rider who seriously wants to be World Champion just has to have Honda as his first choice.

They also set the standards for my other sponsors. I want serious sponsors who have the same attitude as Honda. One side of this will be that they can pay me good money. I get a fee for signing the contract at the end of the year and then bonuses based on results. But just as important for me is that the company has the right image for me. All my equipment is the best, or as good as the best, in the world and that's important for a young rider. As I get older – and hopefully more successful – I want to have my own race gear under the Dave Thorpe label. That's a dream at the moment but it's something we're looking at for the future.

Wednesday is the day when I try to meet any journalists who want to see me. I get on really well with the press and look upon most journalists as my friends. My regret is that my only language at the moment is English. I admire Barry Sheene's fluency in foreign languages and this must be a great help in getting your ideas across to people from different countries. It would also be more polite for me to speak another language instead of expecting all journalists to speak English. This winter, Sharon and I are going to try and find the time to start night school and learn at least one new language.

Thursday is not my favourite day! The one thing I don't like about my job is the travelling and Thursday is travelling day. If I could have a magic carpet and just arrive at the race two seconds after leaving home, I'd be a happy man. But still, it's got to be done.

You must understand that I work for the Honda Racing Corporation and they are interested in one thing only: winning the World Championship. This means that these sixteen races take priority over all else and they also mean travelling a lot, since only two of the sixteen are in Britain. It is just as important for me to win the World Championship but I am also keen to do well in Britain. After all, I'd be

nowhere without British racing. That's why I take the British Championship so seriously. It's also very good for Honda UK and certainly Gerald Davidson (Head of Honda UK), likes me to do well.

Anyway, back to travelling. I always let dad get to the meeting first since he's really choosy about where the van is parked. Me, I couldn't care less but you know, wherever I park, dad will want to move so I let him arrive first. He once had us drive twice round the paddock looking at all the empty spaces and it was only on the third lap that he decided exactly where we should be. Providing we're not right next to the track so that dust gets into the salad, I'm happy anywhere.

Friday. I'm naturally a very relaxed person. It took me some time to realise that this is not only good for me but also my sponsors too. Some riders need to shut themselves off from the world before a race but I like to meet people. I don't consider myself anything special as a person and I certainly don't think I have the right to be big-headed or off-hand with the fans, so I always find time to chat to them.

This has proved very useful for my sponsors. After all, the more exposure I get, the better it is for them. But another useful thing has happened. I try very hard to treat every race the same. You know, it would be very bad for me to start thinking that this race is really important and that race isn't. Obviously, a mid-week International isn't nearly so important as a Grand Prix but getting all wound up about a G.P. isn't the way to win. So I chat to the fans, go and see the other riders and gossip to the press and trade. Just generally relax, see what's happening and try to feel comfortable, in the surroundings.

Fortunately, Sharon and I both like food. All food, no matter where we are. When I'm away, we might eat the local delicacy and if I feel like it, I'll have a glass of lager or wine. I'm quite keen on Asti Spumante at the moment. I'm not the sort of person who needs alcohol but I don't have to ban it either. The key thing for me is to behave as nearly as possible as if I'm at home. Relaxed, happy and calm. Then I'm ready to race.

My last job of the day before going to bed is getting my goggles ready. Nine pairs of clear and nine pairs of tinted is the usual – plus tear-offs.

Saturday. This is really the start of the race although it will be another 24 hours before we actually compete. Let me explain how the Honda Team is organised. First of all, my job is to ride the bike. That's all. We have two engine technicians and two chassis engineers from Honda plus two Showa designers. Showa actually own the suspension on the bike. Their job is to develop it continually. They do too! The bike is much quicker now, (July 1984), than it was in March. And although it hasn't changed very much from last year, it's a lot better bike.

Each rider has a mechanic and his job is to make sure that the bike is running properly and is set up to the rider's preference. I don't change my bike a lot. I prefer to set it up at the start of the season and then just perfect my riding. Andre (Malherbe) is really keen. He has a notebook for every track and is continually testing and trying to improve the bike. He might try nine rear tyres before deciding what to use for the race. I'm a lot easier to please.

One day, when I've got more experience and I've won the World Championship, I would like to do development work like Andre does. For me, he's the best rider ever. So technical and intelligent and such a hard competitor. He's really the best. But for now, I've got to concentrate just on being World Champion and trust people with more experience to help me with the technical side of racing.

The pressure is always on the Champion.

*Below :* Everyone wants to talk to a World Champion. Dave is naturally charming and presents a superb image for both himself and motocross.

Saturday is just for free training and at first, I'll just cruise round. I don't walk the tracks any more, although I used to be dead keen on this. Perhaps I'm just getting lazy!

There's a sort of game which goes on between the good riders. If a quick bloke gets behind you in practise, you've either got to drop him quickly or pull over and let him lead. If you have a big go and he stays with you, he's got the psychological advantage. If you can do this to him, then you win. He might also show you a new line, which you hadn't worked out. Talking about lines, I practise on a variety of them. Not only the fastest line but also the smoothest for when I get tired or unusual lines so that I can pass anywhere.

Sunday. Race day. The reason for the rest of the week so far as I'm concerned. As I've said, I don't let race day get on top of me. For instance, half an hour before I won at Hawkstone, I was signing autographs and having my picture taken with the fans. I really do enjoy being with them and I'm grateful for their support. It really does mean a lot to me.

I have a meal before racing. Not a huge amount but enough so I won't feel hungry and then I get changed. I'm not usually bothered about timed training as long as I'm somewhere in the first bunch. The only time I have ever been bothered was at Hawkstone. A lot of people – even in the Honda Team – didn't think I could win there but I knew I could. So, at the start of timed training, I did a really quick lap and then sat back and watched everyone else try and get near it. That really worried some riders – including Jobe who had written me off in a magazine article the week before. He was seven seconds slower, which put the pressure on him, not me.

**Dave doing what he does best.**

The only time I ever get nervous is the few minutes when we're in the parc ferme with the bikes before the first moto! I can't stop going to the toilet and sometimes this can be really embarrassing! At Hawkstone, with two million people watching and two minutes before the race, off I have to go to the toilet! You can't get more embarrassing than that!

The starts don't worry me but I'm always glad when we're through the first corner. This is the one part of the race where you can get into trouble through no fault of your own. You know how I've been saying that I never get annoyed? Well in Switzerland last year, I could have killed Kurt Nicoll when he took me out on the first corner. The whole race was over in just a few seconds and it was nothing to do with me. It's one of the few times I've ever been really angry with someone in a race. Still, Kurt and I are the best of mates now.

Once the race is really under way, all the training and practising starts to pay off. Each race is very different so I can't describe one as being typical. Dad keeps me informed about what is happening with the pit board and I know that I'm good enough to beat most of the riders I race against most of the time. The hard thing is to beat **ALL** the riders and with my Honda team mates and Carla, that's never easy.

In training, I've worked out all the lines I can use so I can get past someone almost everywhere it's possible to pass. I've got a reputation for passing cleanly and I like that. Apart from anything else, if you pass a bloke easily, you make it clear to him that you can outride him and he isn't so keen at having a go at you. The only time I would ever stick my neck out is in the last few laps of a G.P. when I really need the points. Although I never worry about getting hurt – like most top riders, I have enough confidence in my own ability not to think about crashing – you do need bottle. If it comes to the crunch, then I'll have a go even if there is only a 50/50 chance of getting away with it.

I don't want you to think that I pass like this all the time or that I like taking chances, but motocross is a hard sport and if winning is important to you, then sometimes you've got to have a really big go. If you can't bring yourself to do this now and again then you're never going to do really well. For me, doing well means only one thing. Being World Champion. I've won plenty of championships before now and I've been pleased with everyone but until I've shown that I am the best rider in the world, I'll never be completely happy."

## Postscript

Because it takes such a long time to put a book together, this chapter was written a long time before Dave became World Champion. Not that reaching the top has made the slightest difference to his attitude. He is just as totally dedicated and ruthlessly professional about his racing now as he was when he was working his way up to be World Champion. He's also just as nice a person: polite, helpful and that rarest of things in a World Champion, a genuinely nice human being. Dave and I decided to squeeze in this short postscript to bring the book up to date as we went to press. By the time you are reading this, I am sure that Dave will be well on his way to his second World Championship.

"One of the worst meetings of the year was the British Championship at Howe Hills. This was just a week before the final Grand Prix at Wohlen, in Switzerland, and the problem was that I wanted to ride my best at Howe Hills but I had the Wohlen on my mind all the time.

The people in the North-East don't get to see much top-class motocross so I wanted to ride really well for them. It's my job to ride well but they are so keen up there that I wanted to put on a really good show. But all the time, I was thinking, what if I have a silly accident and miss the World Championship.

Mark Banks was going really hard so I hope that we made a good show and I won without taking any chances and that made me happy. Then all the fans were wishing me good luck and that made me feel real good. I do appreciate what they do for me.

So we went to Wohlen and everybody was saying — just ride for points and you'll be okay. Even my dad was telling me to take it easy. But I knew what I had to do and I also knew what was best for me. I know how to race in the way which is easiest for me and the easiest way to win the World Championship for me was to go out and beat everybody. That's all there was to it but I couldn't explain that to anyone in case they thought I was being over-confident.

I had already decided I wanted to be World Champion. I mean, not dreamed about being the best but honestly decided. When I saw them throwing Carlqvist in the air at St. Anthonis in 1983, I thought, 'That's for me!' If you decide that you want to do something and you believe that you **can** do it then, if you have a little bit of luck, you can do it. From then on, I knew I was going to be World Champion.

After training, I knew that I was the fastest man there and I knew I could win. Leif Persson led from the start but I went by him without too much trouble. Then Andre tried to come by but he didn't have the answer. He had two or three big goes and after that we both knew he was beaten.

That left the final leg and really, I only had to tour round. Andre passed me at the jump just by the start and I just let him go. I knew I could beat him if I wanted but now my mind was just on something stupid going wrong. I was sure that the bike would be perfect mechanically but there are some things you can't control, like a gear lever getting ripped off in one of the deep ruts or a chain breaking and jamming the rear wheel. There's so many little things which can ruin a race, especially at a muddy meeting.

I was third for about 20 minutes and then I let Georges, Kurt and Eric go through. I wasn't worried about them racing me but I was frightened they might come off and bring me with them. The last few laps seemed to last like hours. All the time, I was watching that I didn't hit a rock and break a rim or rip something off in a rut. Then it was over and I was World Champion. Or should I say we were World Champion. Me, dad and Honda. It felt really, really good."

# Index